Summers at the Lake
Upper Michigan Moments and Memories

Jon C. Stott
Photography by Deb Le Blanc

Modern History Press

Ann Arbor, MI

ISBN 978-1-61599-669-8 paperback
ISBN 978-1-61599-670-4 hardcover
ISBN 978-1-61599-671-1 eBook

Published by
Modern History Press
5145 Pontiac Trail
Ann Arbor, MI 48105

www.ModernHistoryPress.com
info@ModernHistoryPress.com

Tollfree 888-761-6268
FAX 734-663-6861

Distributed by Ingram (USA/CAN/AU), Bertram's Books (UK/EU)

Audiobook available Audible.com and iTunes

Contents

Table of Figures

Dedication

To the memory of my father and Carol, who both loved "our" lakes—JCS

To the memory of my parents, Ralph and Coral, who loved the Upper Peninsula—DKL

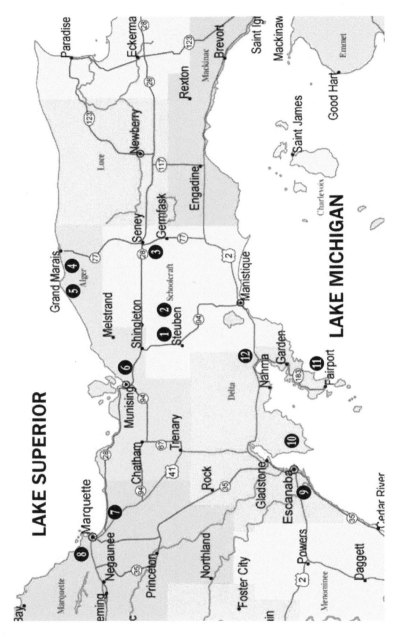

Summers at the Lake Points of Interest

Key to *Summers at the Lake* Points of Interest Map

1. **Colwell Lake** (Introduction; Chapters 1, 2, 4, 5, 8)

2. **Crooked Lake** (Introduction; Chapters 1, 2, 3, 4, 5, 7, 8)

3. **Seney**: Seney National Wildlife Refuge (Chapter 6)

4. **Grand Marais**: Lake Superior Brewing Company at Dunes Saloon, Pickle Barrel Museum (Chapter 6)

5. **Au Sable Point**: Au Sable Light Station (Chapter 6)

6. **Munising**: Sand Point Marsh Trail, East Channel Brewing Company, ByGeorge Brewing Company (Chapters 1, 6, 7, 8)

7. **Lakenenland** (Chapter 6)

8. **Marquette**: Snow Bound Books, Lake Superior Smokehouse and Brewpub, Drifa Brewery, Vierling Restaurant and Marquette Harbor Brewing, Ore Dock Brewery, Blackrocks Brewery, Barrel + Beam Brewery (Chapters 4, 6, 8)

9. **Escanaba**: Hereford and Hops Steak House and BrewPub, Upper Hand Brewery (Chapter 6)

10. **Peninsula Point** (Chapter 8)

11. **Fayette Historical Village** (Chapters 6, 8)

12. **Cooks**: LaTulip Brewery (Chapter 6)

Preface – The Little Cabin in the Big Woods

In 1985, Carol and I bought a cabin beside Crooked Lake in Michigan's Upper Peninsula. We called it "The Little Cabin in the Big Woods." Since then, I, along with family members and close friends, have spent all or parts of extended summers at the cabin. We have enjoyed being on the lake and by its shore, have visited nearby towns, immersed ourselves in the scenery, and benefited from learning about history through the many historic sites.

Most of the essays in *Summers at the Lake* are presentations of memories, moments, and musings of and about people, places, and events that have made Crooked Lake summers so special to me and my family. There are also some comparisons between times at Crooked Lake and the years of my boyhood when summers were spent at Shawnigan Lake on Vancouver Island, British Columbia. I have also included a few of the pieces that my father, Art Stott, a columnist for the *Victoria Daily Times*, wrote about those childhood summers.

No two summers at a lake are the same: the weather can be blisteringly hot one year or miserably moist another; the blueberry crop, a bonanza one year and non-existent another. Old neighbors leave and new ones move in. Children grow up, their youthful enthusiasms replaced by those of their own children. A loon family may survive intact one year, while in another an adult, a chick, or both may be killed. But, underlying these variables, there is an enduring rhythm to a lakeside summer. I have tried to evoke this rhythm in individual pieces and have arranged essays from different years in a way that suggests the natural progression of the seasons. The moments and memories presented here are my own. But I hope that they will evoke for readers memories of similar incidents and feelings at other lakes and at other times.

Introduction – Rainy Day Magic

For the third straight day, it's cold, rainy, and windy at the lake. Only the dogs want to go outside—they are anxious to splash through the puddles that are growing larger on the path to the dock. In spite of the weather, I don't feel grumpy; I recall the old saying that every cloud has a silver lining, and I remember two wonderful times when that saying came true for us.

In late June 1971, we rented a tent trailer and spent our first night camping at a State Park on the Lower Peninsula of Michigan. The weather was fine; we established a very close relationship with our neighbors, whose tent was pitched only a few feet from our trailer; and we increased our stamina by hiking and pushing Clare's overloaded stroller along the bumpy path to the beach, which was over a quarter of a mile away.

That night, Carol brought out a very thick Michigan camping guide she'd bought. "Here's something interesting," she said and then read a short paragraph about a primitive campground at Colwell Lake in an Upper Peninsula National Forest. There were pit toilets and no electricity, but each site fronted onto the water.

The next morning, the weather had turned cold and rainy as we pulled off M-94 and a vigorous north wind was churning Colwell Lake into whitecaps. I stopped in front of a vacant campsite and Carol got out to look around. She walked through the trees toward the lake and when she returned, she was smiling. "We've been looking for this kind of place for years."

The weather didn't improve very much over the next few days, but we knew we'd found our spot. Even when we moved from Kalamazoo to Edmonton, Canada, and the drive to Colwell Lake became two-and-a-half days instead of eight hours, we never wanted to camp anywhere else.

In 1985, we rediscovered the truth about rainy days and silver linings. We'd made the long drive from Western Canada to Colwell Lake where we were meeting up with very close friends—Bob, Barb, and Diane from Kalamazoo and Jan and Craig from Kingston, Ontario.

We'd planned very carefully and, to make the week somewhat luxurious, we rented a motor home from a guy in Marquette. But things didn't work out as smoothly as scheduled. The motor home was a piece of junk: the generator wouldn't hold a charge and so the fridge didn't work, and you need a screwdriver to open the door from the inside. At least it didn't leak. The friend Clare had brought along from Edmonton was not a happy camper, especially when she discovered that there was no electricity for her hair dryer. Then the two of them had a falling out when both developed crushes on the teenage boy camping next door.

And so, on a day like today—cold, rainy and windy—Clare, Craig and Jan, and I decided to take a walk to Crooked Lake, the next one over from the campground. On earlier camping trips, when it was too cold to be at the beach, we'd often walked there and fantasized about how nice it would be to have one of the cabins. We never thought that could happen.

Just as we were about to turn around and head back to the campground, we saw a for-sale sign at the end of a driveway. We knocked on the door of the cabin, asked the owner the price, and, when we found out how low it was, I made an offer on the spot. Our cloud that day did have a silver lining.

Now, I try never to complain about wet, windy weather. Because of two rainy days, we've had countless golden moments that have been transmuted into priceless memories.

1   Dreaming and Arriving

In autumn and early winter, after I've closed up camp and returned to Albuquerque, the city of the pavements gray, the lake seems incredibly distant in both time and space, seems almost to be unreal. But in mid-winter, as the days gradually lengthen and the sun's warmth increases, I find myself thinking about the place where I'll be arriving when the snows have melted and the white petals of the service berries have floated gently to the ground. As the countdown to the time of departure begins, I begin planning and preparation. The journey is a happy one, filled with the pleasures of anticipation. The incidents of travel and arrival may vary in details, but emotions stirred are always similar: an increasing excitement of returning to and reconnecting with the life of a place I have loved for so many decades.

Dreaming of Trails

Last night, I sat before a small winter fire watching the flames flicker and then turn into glowing coals. I'd been reading one of my Christmas gifts, Robert Moor's *On Trails: an Exploration*, an interesting collection of autobiographical, historical, descriptive, philosophical and meditative essays structured around an account of his hiking the 2,193 mile Appalachian Trail.

My mind wandered to the Little Cabin in the Big Woods, and I started to doze, dreaming of trails. It frequently happens sometime in January when I realize that in four or five months, I'll be arriving back at Crooked Lake. Then I start envisioning the trails I'll be walking, pedaling, or paddling along when I get there. These won't be major expeditions, just short excursions along familiar paths.

The first path will be down to and then along the lakeshore. I think about the excitement I'll feel as I reach the dock and see how high or

Fig. 1-1: Wild Rose

low the water level is. Then I'll stroll along the shore noticing where the long green blades of the iris plants will soon thrust above the water, bringing their promise of blue flowers to come. I'll check to see if the wild rose bush has made it through the winter, remembering how, many springs ago, I'd go early each morning to pick a bud, bring it home, put it in a brandy snifter, and place it on the table where Carol and I would sit, sipping our coffee and looking out the window at the light of the rising sun playing on the trees across the lake.

Later in the day, I'll pedal my old bike along two different trails. On the first, a two track behind our place, I'll go very slowly, casting my eyes right and left, looking for clumps of blueberry bushes. If I arrive earlier in the season, there will be little white blossoms; if it's later, there will be young berries, hard little green bbs. But I'll be able to forecast how bountiful the harvest will be in late July.

Late in the afternoon, I'll put on my bright yellow safety vest and pedal out to the highway to pick up the *Mining Journal*. If there's not too much traffic and I'm fortunate, I may see reminders I'm biking through a wild forest: a deer bounding across the road ahead of me before crashing through the underbrush; a snapping turtle planting itself defiantly in the middle of the road, glaring angrily as if daring me to pass; a small owl on a branch twisting its head to get a better look at the strange wheeled creature who's going "whoo, whoo" at it.

And finally, I'll imagine a morning when the lake is calm and, for the first time of the season, I'll follow its invisible trails, paddling a few strokes and then gliding through the mist rising from the water, enjoying the aroma of someone's breakfast bacon carried by the slight breeze, feeling the thrill of the sudden and brief appearance of a loon's head, or smiling at the harsh squawks of a far-off sand hill crane, whose laryngitis-like calls belie its stately nature.

My head drops to my chest, my book falls from my hands onto the floor. I snap awake. The fire has turned into embers. I pick up the book, turn out the lights, and head to bed, thinking that in several weeks, these reveries will be realities.

Sounds in the Night

Last night, I was awakened by the piercing and angry snarl of a motorcycle as it jack-rabbited out from a stop sign onto a main Albuquerque street not far away. Had the cyclist many miles to go before he could sleep? Or was he taking joy at killing the peaceful slumbers of people living close to the stop sign?

Twenty minutes later, the mournful wail of a police siren filled the night. Had there been a serious, even fatal auto accident? Had there been yet another murder in this large southwestern city?

And then, not long after, came the POP, POP, POP of gunfire from the place, a few blocks to the east, that the locals call the "War Zone." Had angry words been exchanged in the parking lot of a bar, and had someone tried to punctuate the words of the argument with a Saturday night special? Or had a driver slowed down to fire at the front windows of what he thought was the home of an enemy?

When the quiet returned, I thought about what sounds I might hear if it were late spring and I were awake at a lake so far away.

Perhaps the haunting ululations of a loon would float across the water, as a partner signaled to its mate that all was well and that it would soon be back at the nest to warm the eggs that would crack open with new life in a few days.

Perhaps the leaves of the popple outside my window rustle in the predawn breeze or a pine cone hits the roof with a soft thud and rolls across the shingles and lands on the ground where a few of its seeds might sprout into tiny young trees.

Or perhaps the scolding of a squirrel who is not really scolding, but announcing to whomever it has awakened that the new day was coming and that it was great to be noisily alive.

And, with these sounds in my mind, I drifted back to sleep.

Counting Sleeps

When we were kids, our parents taught us counting songs so that we could learn our numbers – "One, two, buckle my shoe; three, four, shut the door." Then, when Andrew and Clare were little, we used to all chant the ditty from "Sesame Street" – "One, two, three, four, five, watch the bees go in the hive." Over six decades ago, my sisters and I amused ourselves in the car by tallying out-of-state license plates. Most were from Washington, Oregon, and California, but once I proudly spotted one from some place called Michigan.

Now that I'm entering my second childhood, I'm reverting to counting games. I've invented one called "Counting Sleeps." That's not a typo. I'm like an impatient, excited little kid calculating how long it will be until Santa arrives.

My count doesn't begin in November and it's not about Christmas. It usually begins in very early spring, as the days are getting longer and warmer, and it's about arriving back at the lake that I'd left many long months ago. By the end of September it seemed like I've been gone forever and that my return was ice ages away. In March, there may be ice on the lake, but I can already imagine it when the sun is glinting off the water and the fishermen are casting from boats, not huddling in fishing shanties around holes cut in the ice.

I try to be patient and usually start by counting the sleeps left only once a week. But when the anticipation is too great, I drift to sleep imagining that there are no sleeps left and that I'm passing through Green Bay for the last four hours of a drive that began three days earlier. I see us putting into Jack's Market in Manistique, buying just enough supplies to last for the days I'll be recovering from the trek. I see the turnoff from M-94 to the road winding through the forest toward the cabin.

Hankie is leaning his labradoodle head out the car window, sniffing intently. I park behind the cabin and open the car door. He leaps out and tears around in circles, releasing energy pent up during the long trip. I pause, listening to hear if there's a nasty mosquito buzzing next to my ear.

Even before unpacking, I head down to the lake to see how well the dock has weathered the winter and how high the water level is. Then I unlock the door and smell the mustiness of the long-closed interior and begin to unpack the supplies of summer: clothes, books, notes, paper, writing supplies, food, and some craft beer from New Mexico or that I've picked up along the way.

The images in my head can't change the fact that it's still March and that there's still ice on the lake. I've got lots to get done and miles to drive before I have my first sleep at the cabin. But sometimes the reveries of anticipation get me so excited that I have trouble getting to sleep.

Here ... and There

I'm watching a black-chinned hummingbird hovering in front of the flowers of the yellow bird-of-paradise shrub just outside my office window in Albuquerque. And I'm thinking of a ruby-throated hummingbird hovering in front of the screen porch at the lake, checking to see if I've refilled the feeder.

I see the tiny lavender-blue flowers of the Russian sage out by the sidewalk. And I'm thinking of the rich blue and purple irises that, in mid-June, will be in full bloom in the swamp beside the road.

Hankie and Trina are tearing around raising great clouds of dust in the backyard. Soon they'll be water-buffaloing and water-gazelling in the shallows of Crooked Lake.

I can hear the chimneysweep on the roof getting the fireplace ready for late autumn in New Mexico when the cool evenings will be made cozy by the cheery flames and the crisp outside air will be scented by pinon smoke. Then I imagine an evening campfire by the lake, with maple and birch crackling and family and friends softly sharing stories and trying not to burn marshmallows while dodging the shifting smoke and slapping at mosquitoes.

Outside, a flock of pigeons (those sheep of the avian world) are lined up along the power cables and cooing. But, in my mind's ear, I hear the early morning call of a loon as it searches for breakfast.

In the midst of a very large city in the high desert of the southwest, I think of a little northern fishing lake and the Little Cabin in the Big Woods. As it was for William Wordsworth when he remembered the fields of daffodils in his beloved Lake District of England, "my heart with pleasure fills." I realize that ruby-throated hummingbirds, irises, campfires, splashing dogs, and loons will soon be a reality.

Preparations

Long ago, when our family lake place in western Canada was only one very long hour away from town, preparing to go to the cabin was a fairly simple matter. My mother would pack a box of groceries (most were canned or packaged) and a duffel bag of clothes (camp wear that included tired jeans, frayed tee shirts, and down-at-the-heel running shoes). We'd be responsible for whatever books or toys we wanted to bring along. There was no need to have the water system activated or the telephone and long distance. The water system was me and two buckets and there was no telephone and no electricity. If we'd left anything behind, our father would bring it with him next weekend.

Now that the lake I go to is a three-and-a-half day drive away and I spend all the summer there, the preparations are more detailed and careful. I begin them two or three weeks before departure: calls to the plumber and handyman to start the water system and remove the heavy shutters from the windows and screen porch, and notifications to the phone company to have the internet and long-distance plan activated and to Brenda at the *Mining Journal* to begin delivery on the day I arrive. I've been sorting and packing clothes, some well-on in years that will be used when I do some house painting, some for the really hot days (not many of those) and more for the damp, rainy ones and the chilly mornings. Then some food staples that are not available in the UP: Desert Seasonings, packets of New Mexico style spices for dips, and some Hatch chili (red and green). And I always take along a sampling of local craft brews to bring to our annual share-the-beers night.

But the most important preparation I begin when there are five days to go before I leave. I start growing my summer beard. I begin to look like someone you wouldn't want to meet when you're walking your dog by the dawn's early light. I don't try to look scruffy; it's that I need to have a beard in a week.

That's when I'll be turning down the driveway to the Little Cabin in the Big Woods. There probably won't be anyone around, but just in case there is, I don't want to be mistaken for a prowler. The people at the lake have never seen me without a beard. After a few weeks, it begins to look pretty wild, like I'd been living too long in the wilderness. "Are there any birds nesting in there?" one of the lake's self-styled humorists, who couldn't grow a decent beard if he tried, asked snidely.

One year, near the end of the season, one of the neighbors came over and handed me a small package. "It's a tee shirt I saw when I was down in Grand Rapids. The guy on the front of it reminded me of you," he explained. The guy on the front had a big, floppy hat like the one I wear at the lake; his clothes looked the worse for wear and dirty, just like mine. He carried an ax over his shoulder—a huge, double bitted one, way bigger and more dangerous-looking than my camper's one. And he had a big, wild, and very luxurious beard. Below this portrait was the name of the beer: "Founders Backwoods Bastard Ale."

I still wear it proudly. In fact, it's one of the first pieces of apparel I pack when I'm preparing to head to the lake.

On the Road Again

Early tomorrow morning, as I turn onto Interstate 25 heading north out of Albuquerque, I'll do something I rarely do and object to when other drivers do it. I'll play a song very loudly on the car stereo.

It will be Tom Cochrane's 1991 hit, "Life Is a Highway," and playing it has been part of the yearly trip to Crooked Lake for over a quarter-of-a-century. It began in 1992, when we left from Edmonton and headed eastward. The previous winter had been difficult. We'd spent several weeks in Los Angeles where Carol had been taking treatments for melanoma. They had not been successful.

But we sang along loudly and joyously as we drove out of town and Tom Cochrane's words boomed from the speakers. In two-and-a-half days, we'd be at the place we loved, enjoying the semi-solitude and (usually) the quietness.

During our stay, our friends Jan and Craig would be coming from Ontario, and Clare would be flying in from Alberta. Sometimes the north wind would blow cold from Lake Superior and the mosquitoes might have us slavering bug juice on during the day and covering our heads with bed covers at night so that we won't hear the whine of hundreds of them trying to get through the screens. But we'd have a great time.

Our excitement rose as we came down the hill into Duluth, Minnesota and caught our first glimpse of Lake Superior. Then, two more glimpses as we came down two more hills, into Marquette and then Munising. We were getting closer. And finally, we turned into the dirt driveway leading to the cabin.

This time, I'll be taking a different route to Michigan—from Albuquerque, not Edmonton. There'll be other landmarks to indicate that I'm getting closer to the dirt driveway: the bridges across the Missouri River in South Dakota and the Mississippi at the Minnesota-Wisconsin border. And when I see Lambeau Field looming to my right as I drive through Green Bay, I'll know I've got only four hours to go.

Along the route, I'll hum "Life is a Highway," remembering with a sweet sadness the joys Carol and I experienced on our last drive together to Crooked Lake and the greater ones after we'd turned onto the dirt road.

The Stops Along the Way

When we were kids making the excruciatingly long one-hour trip to Shawnigan Lake, we enjoyed several ritual stops. While my father gassed up the car at the Five Points Service Station, we dashed across the street to Fosters' Store. It had the best selection of comic books for miles around. We would buy one each, and, when one of us was at the counter, the other two would quickly read another while the owner was distracted. Forty minutes later, we'd stop at the Malahat Chalet to buy popsicles, which we'd try to make last for the remaining 15 minutes of the journey. They never did, although we'd each claim to have made ours last longer than the others'.

As we neared the south end of the lake, we'd compete with each other to see who would be the first to spot the lake. Like holding the last number of a rotary phone dial until the quiz question was announced on the radio, we would very slowly say, "I.....I..... s-e-e-e-e-e ... the l-l-l" and then shriek out the last syllable: "AKE!" There'd be some more arguments, often very fierce ones, over who'd uttered "ake" first.

My father slowed down when we reached the rise that overlooked "our" bay. Sometimes we could see our cousins playing on the beach in front of the cabins. He would give a ritual tooting of the horn: one long, two short, one long, one short and one long to announce our imminent arrival. We'd turn off the main road, drive the half mile of what we called the "bumpity road," with my father expertly navigating the exposed rocks that could have taken out the oil pan. As the car came to a stop, we flew out from the back seat and headed toward the lake. Then came the final part of the ritual. My father would call out firmly, "Stop! We still have to unpack the car and take stuff into the cabin." We reluctantly trudged back, did our duty, and then raced to see our cousins.

Now the trip to the lake is longer—1917 miles and three-and-a-half days. But there are still rituals to be observed. We have favorite restaurants we patronize. We even have favorite rest areas: ones that have lots of shade to park the car and a place to walk the dogs that isn't too close to other cars and semis: like the one outside of Lusk, Wyoming, which is reportedly the first rest area in the United States, or the one just after LaCrosse, Wisconsin, which is located where there was once a lake created by melting glaciers, or the one after Escanaba, Michigan, which has a great view of Lake Michigan and is just over an hour from our destination.

When we cross the Interstate Bridge from Marinette, Wisconsin to Menominee, Michigan, I always call out, "Hello, Michigan! We're back!" There's usually nobody around when I arrive at our driveway, but I still honk the horn: one long, two short, one long, one short, one long. I open the doors to the backseat of the car and the dogs rush down to the lake.

I'm left to unpack the car all by myself.

Breakfast on the Road

For over half a century, it's been a family tradition, when we make long road trips, to start early (it used to be 4:30, now it's around 6:00 am), to drive a fair distance (formerly 150 miles, now 60) and then stop to enjoy a hearty breakfast. After a couple of difficult experiences, we learned to go easy on the coffee. It's often a long way between rest areas and, on the prairies, there are no trees and the bushes are rather small.

Over the years, some of the restaurants on our regular routes have become favorites. They have two things in common: they have good food AND they're local. Of course, it's hard to do a really bad job of cooking breakfast, although I once stopped at a local place that did an excellent job of being really bad, and dirty, and with rude and incompetent servers. It had the audacity to include the word "cuisine" on the big sign towering above the paper-strewn parking lot.

Local is important. When you go in, you look for a table where three or four retirees are sitting. Then you pick a table behind them and sit with your back to them. If you listen intently, you'll learn lots of town gossip: who's just lost a job, whose adult child is leaving her jerk of a husband, why the high school team should get a new coach for the fall. You also learn interesting interpretations of national and international politics—who should be booted out of office, who is the worst of the candidates running in the upcoming primary. If you're a fisherman (and I'm not), you can discover where the best spots are, what's biting, what's the best bait or lure to use, what's the best time to head out on the water.

This year, one of my favorite stops, Pancho's in Las Vegas, New Mexico, held a special interest. A few weeks ago, Clare had called me to look at the movie she was watching "No Country for Old Men" There, sitting at our table at Pancho's, discussing a major plot complication, were Tommy Lee Jones and a colleague.

I stopped there on my way to Michigan. As I ordered my usual—ham well done, eggs easy over, wheat toast, go easy on the coffee—I talked with Gene, the owner, about the movie. "It was only a five minute scene," he remarked. "But they were here for three days—one to set up, one to film, and one to clean up." One of the employees was in the background of the scene working behind the counter. But Gene wasn't. "I'm 6 foot 8," he explained. "And Tommy Lee Jones is only six one. I'd have been too tall for the camera angles they wanted." He remembered that Jones was rather standoffish, but that the other cast members were quite friendly. "It's funny; the most friendly was Javier Bardem." Gene chuckled. "And he played the psychotic killer."

In a couple of months or so on the way back from Michigan, I'll be stopping there again. Clare will be with me and we'll ask Gene to take a picture of the two of us. When we show it to our friends, we'll tell them that, in 2007, Tommy Lee Jones sat at our table.

Arrival!

As I turned off M-94 and began the two mile drive through the woods, the anxious excitement of earlier this morning increased faster than the speedometer in the car of a Saturday night street racer.

I turned into the driveway and "sighed a heave of relief," as my grandfather used to say. The Little Cabin in the Big Woods was still there! You could tell I'd been away for a long time. The rotten branch of a small birch stretched across the driveway. Branches from the spruce tree, untrimmed for nearly three years, now hung low, scraping the car as I passed. Leaves "no step had trodden black" carpeted the ground. There was a blanket of pine needles on part of the roof.

When I came inside, I soon discovered that after the winter, the routine maintenance chores had piled up. The plywood subflooring leading to the bathroom had rotted and become spongy and the sump pump that drained the septic tank wasn't functioning properly. The telephone company had forgotten to switch on the long distance service and the satellite system wouldn't pick up the signal because of the maple sapling that had grown up in front of it. Those were all problems I'd worry about tomorrow.

When I arrived, the old thermometer nailed to the side of the shed read 76 degrees. It was sunny and a warm breeze was blowing from the south. I quickly unpacked my groceries and donned my baggy old bathing suit and walked down to the lake. The water was a brisk 68; but I waded in, pushed off, took a few strokes underwater and quickly returned to the dock. I felt refreshed; the plunge had washed away the weariness and tensions of a winter spent in a large southwestern city.

Walking back to the cabin, I spotted clumps of powder-blue forget-me-nots, yellow violets, and purple gay-wings pushing up from the carpet of leaves, the tiny, but hardy heralds of spring, the promisers of longer days and warmer weather to come that also evoked sweet memories of opening the cabin years earlier.

I followed the first swim with two other rituals of arrival: the first beer and the first meal. Originally, on the day of arrival, the beer had been one of the "value priced" (i.e., cheap) brands of the brewery giants and the food something like wieners and beans that we could prepare quickly. But in recent years, we've tried something new and something old. The new was a beer from one of the craft brewers that had recently begun operations. This time it was "Maize-in-Grace," a light lager from Munising's By George Brewery, which wasn't open last fall. The old was a pasty, a hand pie that had been introduced to the UP by Cornish miners in the middle of the 19th century. Mine contained rutabaga, potato, onions, carrots, and beef nested in a pop-

Fig. 1-2: Another picture-perfect sunset over Crooked Lake

over pastry and was made by Muldoons' Pasties, a popular Munising tourist stop that even the locals think is one of the best around.

Tired though I was, I returned to the dock after dinner and sat on the wooden love seat that Carol and I had bought in Edmonton many years ago. Bathed by the rejuvenating breeze from the south, I watched the sun descend to the tree line across the lake. The quiet was broken by the thrilling ululations of a loon and, a few minutes later, by the appearance of a mating pair swimming slowly down the lake only a stone's throw from the dock. It would probably be a few weeks until they again swam together, this time with their chicks. The cycle of nest building, brooding, and feeding young hatchlings was about to begin.

A solitary fisherman, who had been casting along the far shore, turned his boat toward home. A lone bird offered his evensong in full-throated ease. The sun set. As I walked back to the cabin, a single frog belch from the reeds hinted at the late evening choruses that would begin in a few days.

Other Arrivals

Arrivals aren't always perfect. Sometimes the cabin isn't in top shape and there are unexpected incidents, like the time I turned the tap on and three mice scrambled out of the drain pipe and started scurrying around the sink. Another time, after I'd checked that the stove and fridge were working and the water pump and heater operational, I checked the two most important things—the satellite TV connection and the connection to the internet. The TV was fine, but when I turned on the computer—

It didn't work!

What was I to do? I couldn't check my email (including the messages that offered well-paying jobs as soon as I graduated—from high school or college they didn't say—or a wonderful and terrific life of love and friendship from a beautiful and lonely lady who lived far across the sea). I couldn't look at my sports websites, or *ERBZINE*, an on-line magazine that each week featured old Tarzan comics from the 1950s.

So I called Hiawatha Telephone Company, who said to come by after noon the next day and they'd give me new equipment.

That was 18 hours in the future! It started raining outside; there was nothing good on TV. And so I filled in my first evening with an unusual activity—I read a book.

Of course, the weather hasn't always been welcoming when I arrived. One time, as I turned off the highway onto the dirt road that led to the cabin, gray clouds hung low in the sky. On the ground, deep wide puddles that stretched across the road bore evidence of what must have been a recent downpour.

It started to drizzle. I pulled into the driveway and opened the car doors. The dogs, wired after three plus days in the car leapt out. Mosquitoes rushed in to fill the void.

By the time I'd finished unpacking, the rain had turned from a drizzle to a shower. I got soaked. The wind from the north had increased and the ripples on the lake had turned into whitecaps. The dogs, after swimming and rolling in the sand, scratched at the door and, when I opened it, charged in and dried themselves by more rolling—this time on the carpet.

The shower had become a hard rain, but I didn't care. For me the sun was shining. After ten month's living far, far away, I was back at the lake.

2 Right Around Home ... Work and Play

"This isn't a resort," our mother would remind us when we were slow at beginning and finishing our chores at the lake. They were minimal. I chopped kindling for the wood stove and hauled buckets of water from the lake. (Seventy years ago you could drink the water without boiling it.) The rest of our time involved playing cowboys, starting pickup baseball games in the parking lot, reading, paddling our kayaks and swimming.

The activities haven't changed much over the decades. Our Little Cabin in the Big Woods isn't a resort either. It's where we live nearly four months every year. I still chop wood, but I don't have to haul buckets of water. I (fairly) regularly dust, vacuum, and clean the windows. But I do get to read, mess around in boats, swim, pick blueberries, and ride my bike out to the highway to collect the mail and the *Mining Journal*, things I couldn't do if I endured the summer in the city of the pavements gray.

The Woodpile, the Woodman, and the Wolves

I'd just finished unpacking the car yesterday, putting the clothes in drawers and on hooks and the groceries in the fridge, when I heard what sounded like what we used to call a "rattle-trap" pull into the driveway. It was the woodman in a very old pickup truck that seemed to be held together by baling wire. I rushed out, put up my hand to stop him, and moved my car.

"Sorry I'm late," he said. "Flat tire and I had to borrow a tire and wheel from the neighbor." He wasn't late; in fact, he was a day early. If he hadn't been what he called late, he wouldn't have found anyone here. When I mentioned that, he muttered something about having written the date down on last year's calendar. "But it wouldn't have mattered if you hadn't been here. I could have dumped the wood and left the bill tucked into the door. You could have paid me when you arrived."

By the time the woodman had left, it was too late to think about starting to make a woodpile, so I covered the pieces with an old tarpaulin and continued with the rest of my arrival-day duties and rituals.

This morning, after I'd walked the dogs, I started the process of stacking yesterday's wood. First, I removed from the woodpile those of last year's logs that still looked in pretty good condition. I'd put them on top of the new logs. Then I began, finding pieces of wood that fit fairly snuggly together and stacking them. Small pieces that looked as though they could easily be split into kindling were put to one side.

While I was working, I thought about a strange conversation the woodman and I had had yesterday. After he'd finished unloading the truck, he noticed the dogs in the window and wanted to meet them. He patted the pirouetting pooches and then looked seriously at me. "You'd better be careful when they're outside. There are lots of wolves around." He said that there were over 1,200 of them in the UP and then added, "The DNR [Department of Natural Resources] will tell you that there are only about 650, but don't believe that."

He went on to tell me that they were killing so many deer that the population had become dangerously low. "The DNR says it's because of two severe winters in a row. But the wolves are ruining the hunting season." Even worse, he continued, was the fact that the wolves had killed twelve bear-hunting dogs. (The DNR lists only eight kills in the area.) "The wolves are really ruining the bear hunting season."

Then he gave me some advice: "After they've got all the deer, the wolves are going to start after the dogs. And who's next after that? So, if you go out into the woods, be sure to take your gun with you." I didn't tell him that I didn't own a gun.

I thought, as I finished the woodpile and covered it with a tarp against the rain that had begun to fall, that the best thing is to avoid the wolves' territory as I'm sure they'll avoid mine. And if I do see one nearby, I'll go inside with the dogs, light a cozy fire with the new wood, and call the DNR.

Simple Pleasures

I usually start the summer with lots of clean clothes—the newer ones I've brought with me and the ones I laundered just before I left last year. But every few weeks, the chest of drawers starts looking empty and there are a lot of hangers without clothes in the closet. That happened yesterday. So, I bundled up all the dirty ones and headed to the laundromat in town. I brought a bag of quarters, a book, and settled in for the morning. I struck up a conversation with a woman who was dressed far more fashionably than I was.

"What do you do?" asked the woman after I had told her I spent extended summers at a little cabin in the big woods.

"I lead a simple life. I rake and I row, and, when the weather's bad, I read and I write."

"Oh!" she responded, apparently quite unimpressed. As she finished folding her laundry, she told me that she and her husband were headed to Sault Ste. Marie where they'd booked a boat tour of the locks. Early next week, they planned to visit the Henry Ford Museum in Dearborn, in the Lower Peninsula, and, after that they'd cut across southern Ontario to Niagara Falls, where they had booked a helicopter tour. She said good-bye, gathered her basket of laundry, and walked to a large motor home that was too big to park in the lot in front of the laundry.

Later that afternoon, as I sat on the dock facing a warm breeze that was just enough to keep the flies and mosquitoes from landing, I thought about my morning conversation and about my simple life at the cabin and its great joys.

…rising before dawn one morning and watching the pale yellow moon sinking toward the western tree line, its reflection casting a dappled pathway across the water to the dock…

…lighting the morning fire with kindling and starter pieces that had warmed me when I chopped them yesterday afternoon, and then watching the dancing flames as I sipped my coffee…

…hearing the raucous cry of a sand hill crane in the distance as I slipped my canoe into the water and paddled leisurely across the mirror-calm water, and spotting two bald eagles, one perched on a very tall, thin hemlock, looking regally and haughtily down on me, the other, flying across the bow of my canoe. It was the first time I'd seen two of the majestic birds at the lake…

...back in the cabin, working on a writing project that the hectic life in a large southern city had given me neither the time nor the energy to complete...

...enjoying lunch on the dock, a grilled cheese sandwich made with Limpu (a Finnish name) sourdough with caraway seeds. The bread had been baked a few dozen miles away in the village of Trenary. The small hemlock tree on the bank behind me was decorated with new pale-green tips. Across the lake, a variegated tapestry of green signaled the rapid growth of the maple, alder, and birch leaves...

...after an afternoon nap (someone should write a book called "The Joy of Napping"), it was time for routine chores: raking the leaves; making the grounds around the cabin tidy, but not unnaturally neat; spotting the season's first lady slipper; straightening out the shed (which often looks like Fibber Magee's closet); and chopping more kindling for the next cold morning...

...refreshed by an invigorating dip in the chilly, but not frigid lake, sipping a local craft beer and, the breeze having dropped, hearing faint sounds of civilization—the slapping of a screen door several cabins down the shore, a semi driving along the highway, and, surprisingly, a small helicopter flying above the tree-line...

...heading up to the cabin for a simple late dinner followed by an hour or two reading *Danny and the Boys*, by Robert Traver (the pen name of John D. Voelker, best-known for *Anatomy of a Murder*)...

I knew that I could never trade the simple pleasures of life at the Little Cabin in the Big Woods for any number of cross-country expeditions in a very large, state-of-the-art motor home.

The First Blueberries

This morning I celebrated one of my favorite rituals: the season's first blueberry picking excursion. Since I'd arrived at the lake a few weeks ago, I'd stopped by my secret blueberry patch several times to see how things were going. It was a cool spring and the ripening process was maddeningly slow, but, finally, on Friday, it looked like I could start picking in a few days.

Monday and Tuesday had been warm, but damp and mosquito-y. But that was fine because it would keep other people away from the patch. Wednesday there was a slight drizzle and that was even better. It would keep the bugs off and I'd have no competition from other pickers.

Fig. 2-1: Unripe blueberries

I began my preparations by dressing appropriately, wearing my old, but serviceable tan work pants. It would be easy to spot any ticks I might pick up. Then I donned my heavy work shirt with the high collar and the pockets that were big enough to store my bug repellant, and finally, my beekeeper's hat with the mesh face covering.

I was ready to go; I grabbed the pink sand bucket that, long ago, I'd bought for 50 cents at a street sale in Munising for visiting children who never used it, and a sheet of aluminum foil to cover it. The dogs looked woefully at me as I headed to the door; they weren't welcome to join the expedition. I used to let them come along, but one would sidle up to me and strip a branch of all the berries I was about to pick and the other would come bounding out of the bush, charge past me, and knock the pail over.

I parked the car at the edge of the two track, in a place that would make it visible to cars or pickups coming either direction. It was my way of staking my claim to the half acre or so I was about to enter. I found a spot where the berries were plentiful, sat down in the midst of a clump of two or three bushes and got ready to work.

But first, I enjoyed another ritual. I found the biggest, ripest berry I could, picked it, held it up in front of me and, after admiring it, popped it into my mouth. It was the first fresh blueberry I'd had in two years. Last year, I'd arrived late to the lake and the season was over.

After half an hour, my pail was about a third full and I called it quits for the day. The drizzle had turned into a shower, a mosquito had made it under the mesh of my beekeeper's hat and my back was getting sore. But I was happy; it was a good beginning. There'd be more berry-picking excursions to come.

Back home, I gave each of the dogs a couple of berries and poured the rest out on paper towels spread on a cookie tray, tossing the green ones and picking off stems that were still attached. My harvest amounted to two cups, which I put into two baggies. One would be for muffins when my newly-arrived neighbors dropped over for coffee tomorrow. The other would be frozen and be among the many bags I'd take home at the end of the summer.

Tomorrow's muffins would taste great, but the ones I'd make on Christmas morning from the stash I'd brought home would taste even better. As we enjoyed them with morning coffee and awaited the celebration of opening Christmas gifts, I'd remember the morning when the berries were picked. I'd have forgotten the mosquitoes who tried to feast on me and the rain that had soaked my berry-picking clothes. I'd only remember the joy of celebrating that great ritual: the first berry-picking excursion.

Paper Boy

This afternoon, as I bicycled the two miles out to the highway to pick up the *Mining Journal*, I remembered how, seven decades ago, at a lake near Canada's West Coast, hiking to the highway to pick up the evening paper had been one of my chores.

It was only about a half mile each way, but it could be quite scary, especially if we'd listened to "Inner Sanctum" the night before on my grandmother's big battery radio.

There was no traffic on the dirt road and hardly any on the main road. So it was very quiet, except when a wind blew mournfully through the Douglas firs and dead branches rubbed together emitting rasping and very frightening squeaks.

I would grab the paper and walk back to the cabin, only stopping when it was in sight. Then I'd sit down on a boulder by the side of the road and read the funnies and the sports pages. That way, I wouldn't have to wait until my mother finished reading the paper and then have to fight with my sisters over it.

I was around twelve when I stopped being scared and, in fact, would make sure to arrive at the end of the road at least ten minutes before the paper was scheduled to be delivered. That was the summer that I had first discovered how wonderful it was that girls were different from boys. And that summer, the paper boy was a girl. She was about my age, had shining black hair, and I fell deeply in love. The feeling was not reciprocated. She would mutter "Hi" in response to my enthusiastic greetings, toss the paper to me, and pedal her bike around the curve of the road.

Now, there's no dark-haired beauty waiting to toss me the *Mining Journal*. But there have been other, greater rewards as I go to get the paper: a glimpse of a pine martin as it crossed the dirt road eyeing me warily; the sight of a fawn tentatively and delicately stepping out of the trees, and, one June, the view of a pond filled with newly-blossomed wild irises, their rich powder blue framed by the lush greenery of early summer.

Fig. 2-2: White Tailed Deer

And that's a whole lot better than seeing some 12-year-old girl who probably wouldn't have noticed or cared if I had stopped going out to the end of the dirt road to hear her mutter "Hi."

A Pleasant Detour

This afternoon, on my way out to get the paper, I decided to make a detour through the Colwell Lake campground. It was very quiet—only about a quarter of the sites were occupied and only a couple of these by the giant Fifth Wheels (with generators and satellite dishes) that had so dominated the place during the last few weeks.

I pedaled my bike along the shore trail, stopped at site 15, sat on a bench, looked out over the lake, and remembered. We'd first camped at this site 47 years ago. A few months earlier, we'd rented a tent trailer and made our first trip to the UP, staying five days at Colwell Lake. It was cold and wet and windy, but we knew that this was the spot where we'd always want to camp.

So we bought our own tent-trailer and, on Labor Day weekend took it on its maiden journey, to Colwell Lake. It was sunny and we had four wonderful days. Andrew was three-and-a-half, Clare one-and-a-half. They loved it, except for the evening when a really loud thunder and lightning storm rolled over the lake.

As I sat this afternoon looking out at a couple of people fishing in small boats, I remembered how we'd rented a bass-boat called "Mr. Ed" and that, early one morning Andrew and I had gone out and cast our lines for bluegills. They'd just begun to bite when Andrew had to go back to the campsite to go to the bathroom. When we returned to the lake, the fish had disappeared.

One afternoon, we walked the crude trail around the lake. Clare was in her backpack seat and Carol walked ahead so that she could hold branches back and, if I tripped, catch Clare should she catapult over my head.

Before dinner, we all swam. Then Andrew built sandcastles, while Clare, in her circular walker seat, looked sternly every time he flicked a little water at her. That night we made smores over the campfire, with much of the chocolate never making it into the kids' mouths. They wore fresh outfits when we drove back to Kalamazoo the next morning.

I got on my bike and continued my errand out to get the *Mining Journal*. I'd been feeling a little blah when I had left the cabin, but the memories of that Labor Day weekend at Site 15, Colwell Lake, still fresh and vivid, brought a smile to my face and made the day brighter.

Grocery Lists

I'm makin' a list and checkin' it twice. That's not because I'm getting ready to load a sleigh and set off on a whirlwind one-night journey. It's because it's Wednesday and I'm going to town to shop for the week's groceries. When town is over twenty miles away, you want to make sure you come back with everything you need. No running to the store down the block for an ingredient that probably isn't on the store's shelf. There is no store down the block.

Long ago at another lake, my mother made up a grocery list each Wednesday morning. She was even more careful. We didn't have a car during the week, and we didn't have a fridge, just a "safe" that was kept cool by the evaporation of the water that soaked the burlap covering.

Once the list was completed and double checked, she put it in an envelope, sealed the envelope, addressed it to Cudlip and Cann Grocers, Shawnigan Lake, BC, put on a three cent stamp, and handed the envelope to us, with the firm injunction: "Don't dawdle; if you do, there won't be any dinner tonight!"

We walked as quickly as nine-year-olds could to the little roadside country store. Except for fresh milk, the supply of groceries there was pretty meager. However, there was a little post office. We posted the letter and waited until 11 o'clock, when Mr. Vaulkard, the grocer-post master, put the letters into a mailbag, locked the store up, and started climbing the steep mountain trail that led to the Cliffside Station of the Esquimalt and Nanaimo Railroad.

We'd sometimes follow him up the mountain and watch him attach the mail sack to a kind of gallows. We'd put a penny on the tracks and wait for the whistle of the steam locomotive. It would come around the corner, chuffing and huffing, wheels screeching as it slowed down and neared the gallows. A metal arm would stick out from the door of the mail car, hook the bag into the car and then the train would slowly gather speed. We'd look for our squashed pennies and then follow Mr. Vaulkard down the hill, pick a bottle of pop out of the cooler half filled with gurgling, not very cool water, and head home.

Meanwhile, on the train, the contents of the mailbag had been emptied onto a long table and two men, very quickly and efficiently sorted the letters by destination. Fifteen minutes later, my mother's letter was in a bag that had been tossed out onto the platform of the Shawnigan Lake station. Soon, someone from Cudlip and Cann trotted over to the post office (a block from the station) and picked up our grocery list.

Back at the cabin, we had lunch (Lipton's Chicken Noodle Soup or leftovers, along with a peanut butter sandwich), waited for our "hour" to be up so that we could splash into the lake, read, picked fights with each other, and had skip-the-stones-along-the water competitions before swimming until our lips were blue.

At four-thirty, all frivolous activity stopped. We sat at the dock, quiet for once, as we listened for the chugging sound of an inboard motor—the sign that the grocery delivery was imminent. One of the store assistants would glide the boat to the end of the dock, carefully lift the box of groceries on to the dock and, as he set off to his next stop, admonish us to be careful. We were --usually--as we took stuff to the burlap-covered cooler behind the cabin.

The process was repeated on Saturday, except this time the delivery was an hour later and was made by one of the store's owners. That was because, early in the afternoon, our father had come from town and had brought a dozen beer with him. Alex Cudlip or Shirley Cann arranged their schedule so that our dock was the last stop of the afternoon. My father would be down at the dock with us and, when the boat arrived, he'd bring out two beer that had been resting in the cool water under the dock and he and the owner/delivery man would enjoy their libations. My sisters and I would take the groceries up to the cooler.

Late this afternoon, I'll be sitting on the dock. I won't be waiting for a grocery delivery. I'll have made the twenty or so mile trip into town, done the shopping, and, when I got home, unloaded the car and put the perishables in the refrigerator. But I will be enjoying a craft beer cooled in the old fridge in the shed and I'll remember my father's Saturday afternoon hospitality.

Lakeside Reporter

A year ago, knowing that I could be only at the lake for two weeks, I decided to do without the newspaper, the internet, satellite TV, and radio. The *Mining Journal* only sold subscriptions by the month and for twenty-two dollars a month. If there'd been a carrier, I'd have gladly let him have an eleven dollar tip, but now the paper was delivered by the postal service. I didn't have a mailbox, so I not only missed the paper, but the afternoon bike-ride out to the highway to pick it up.

I'd bailed on the internet as well—a fifty dollar start up fee and another twenty five for two weeks. That also shut me out of online feeds and streaming radio. We can't pick up the NPR station in the woods, and now I wouldn't be able to connect on line.

At least, I thought, there was satellite TV. I could catch the weather channel in the morning and the local and national news at night. But the dish had been knocked way off kilter during the winter storms, and there would be a ninety plus dollar service fee to realign it. Besides, the service people couldn't show up until three days before I was to head back to the southwest. I cancelled my service.

That doesn't mean I didn't get any news. I called Clare back in New Mexico every evening. She provided me with a quick rundown of key events and the weather forecast for the UP. She wasn't interested in sports, so I had no idea of how badly the Tigers were doing or whether the Oilers were still in the Stanley Cup playoffs. (I later learned that the

Tigers continued to perform poorly and that the Oilers were defeated by Winnipeg in four straight games.)

However, I do have eyewitness news. Every morning I walk around the lot and down to the lake and look for any changes that may have occurred over night. Yesterday, on the two-track behind the cabin, I saw a pair of deer, the third in a week, as they bounded into the bush. The relatively mild and snow-free winter had increased the survival rate. This summer there should be many, many fawns timidly following their mothers to the water's edge for a pre-dawn drink.

This morning, only one loon fished its way down the lake. The eggs had been laid and the soon-to-be parents were spelling each other in brooding duties.

By the southern wall of the cabin, the forget-me-nots had expanded from a couple to a couple of dozen clumps. Under the pine trees in the next-door neighbor's lot, purple gay wings, delicate, orchid-like flowers, had miraculously appeared, their purple petals giving a cheerful contrast to the gray pine needles all around. Two days ago they weren't there. There were also more wild strawberry blossoms than I'd seen for many years. Hopefully, in late June, there'll be a yield of more than a small handful of the sweet little berries. Walking down the back road, I discovered several new blueberry bushes, and they looked like they'd provide a bountiful harvest.

Oh yes, the weather. A piece of string hanging from a hook on the lantern post by the water is flipping wildly and whitecaps are racing down to the south of the lake. The forecast: strong winds from the north and well-below average temperatures because of the Lake Superior chill they'll bring with them. Tonight I'll be sitting snug and warm in front of the fireplace.

All this important news! And without buying a subscription, paying a reconnect fee, or getting a service bill from the satellite people!

Summer Reading

Summer has always been a time for reading, first at Shawnigan Lake on Vancouver Island and later at Crooked Lake in Michigan's UP. We didn't have electricity at Shawnigan until I was a young teenager and so no radio, and we didn't get a television up there until I was an adult returning with my young family for summer visits.

Fig. 2-3: Blue Iris

Until the last few years in the UP (we recently got a dish and the internet) we had only one TV station which, unless you liked "The Price is Right" or were keeping count of how many robberies were reported on the evening news from Green Bay, wasn't very interesting. So we read, inside on rainy days, on the dock on dry days.

Carol used to stay out on the dock even when the winds were blowing from the north. But, one time they were really fierce, with whitecaps nearly a foot high racing past the end of the dock. Carol wasn't there and she wasn't inside. Had she been blown away? It turned out she'd taken a folding chair behind the cabin, well out of the wind, and was reading there – right over the septic tank. The grass wasn't greener, but at least the wind was closer to being a strong breeze.

In the summer I often enjoy binge reading. I was in third grade when my grandmother used to clip the *Burgess Bedtime Stories* (Old Mother West Wind, Grandfather Frog, etc.) out of the paper and each Saturday my father would bring them up to the lake. I'd read one a day and was ready for a new batch the next week.

Then there was that rainy summer when I must have gone through a dozen or more Bobbsey Twins books. Some of them were pretty old; they were my aunt's favorite books from her childhood. In one Nan and Bert and Freddie and Flossie arrived at a country railroad station from which they were conveyed to a farm by horse and buggy.

This year, just before I left Albuquerque for the summer, I was giving my office bookcases their once-in-a-long-while dusting when I came across *The Collected Works of William Shakespeare*, edited by G. B. Harrison. Over half-a-century ago, it had been the textbook for a couple of Shakespeare courses I'd taken at university. It was somewhat battered: several strips of electrician's tape kept the cover on and the binding together.

Except for a few plays I'd taught in freshman English classes, I hadn't read much Shakespeare since college days. Why not binge-read Shakespeare this summer, starting at the beginning and working my way through to "The Tempest"?

And so, a few days after I'd opened up, I sat in our new screened porch and began reading from the beginning, "The First Part of King Henry the Sixth." It was tough going, an apprenticeship work, as they say. If I hadn't known of the greatness that lay ahead for Shakespeare, I'd have muttered to myself, "I sure hope he didn't quit his day job." I got through it and began "The Second Part of King Henry the Sixth," hoping that his skills had improved.

They hadn't. I made it to the end of Act II, scene iii, put my bookmark in between pages 154 and 155 and closed the book.

"Thank goodness I'm going to Marquette, tomorrow," I said to myself. "Maybe at Snowbound Books, I'll find a Jim Harrison I've overlooked or one of the early Allende novels I read so long ago that I've forgotten what it's about."

At the end of the summer, when I packed the books that were going home, the bookmark was still in place between pages 154 and 155 of *The Collected Works of William Shakespeare*.

Rainy Days at the Lakes

It is a cold, gray day at the lake. We haven't seen the sun for two days. The temperature is hovering around 55 degrees. The water is a slate gray dappled by whitecaps frothed up by a cold north wind. The dogs are sodden from running through deep puddles left from yesterday's four-hour downpour.

I remember long ago summer rainy days at another lake far away. After doing our morning chores—mine involved chopping extra wood to keep the fire going against the damp and chill—we'd read. There was no radio, TV, or even electricity. Then, just before lunch, our desperate mother would make us take a vigorous swim to burn off energy. Usually the water was warmer than the air.

In the afternoon, we'd sometimes pile into the family car and go to the little village where there was a store that sold comic books and a coffee shop where we'd buy a root beer float -- with three straws please.

Then it was back to the cabin. I'd chop more wood, and, after I'd finished the comic book I'd bought, I'd work on my "novel." It was about Squirrel Man, a Tarzan-like hero who killed dangerous cougars and grizzly bears and discovered strange civilizations just beyond the hills on the far side of the lake. I never finished it.

Then it was time for another swim and dinner.

I realized today that the rainy day rituals haven't changed that much. This morning I chopped extra wood, lit a cheery fire, did some research, and read some articles online. In the afternoon I went to town and stopped by Falling Rock to buy *And Here* (a collection of writings from Michigan's Upper Peninsula). Then I picked up a six pack of IPA from Munising's new brewery, East Channel, and came home.

I dozed off reading the book, awoke with a start, relit the fire, and decided I should do some writing, have a swim, put dinner in the oven, open one of the beers, and turn on the TV.

So, I started up the computer.

Here's how I began: "It is a cold, gray day at the lake."

The Joys of Lethargy

Just before dinner yesterday, I made a to-do list of tasks that were long overdue: spending a couple of hours working on the index to my book, walking Trina out to the bridge (a mile away) and back, vacuuming the rug which had become white with her shed fur, and a few other things.

This morning, I slept in until 8:30, two hours past my normal rising time. As I put the coffee in the basket, I noticed the list on the counter, muttered "Mañana," and put an extra scoop in the basket and added more water.

I sat in the screened porch, drank my coffee, read yesterday's paper (old news is good news, maybe), and listened to "Classical Music for a Sunday Morning" on my I-Pad.

When Trina scratched at the door and looked imploringly at me, I gave her an abbreviated walk. She came back with her tail curled and wagging and, as soon as she got inside, flung herself on the carpet, lay on her back and writhed vigorously, leaving more clumps of white hair.

Time for another cup of coffee.

I'd planned to make myself a big Sunday breakfast: bacon, scrambled eggs with cheese, toast and jelly. But I settled for Cheerios. I used a throw-away bowl to cut down on the washing.

Then I wandered down to the shore and surveyed the water weeds that had increased in number this year. I wasn't expecting any young company until next summer, so I didn't need to clean a swimming area in the shallows. A winter's wait wouldn't hurt.

I sauntered back to the cabin, poured what was left of the coffee, then sat in the screened porch and began reading a book I'd brought from Albuquerque but hadn't yet opened.

Three minutes later, I was asleep in my chair.

Lake Dancing

Jan and Craig, who'd camped with us in 1985 when we found our Little Cabin in the Big Woods, will be visiting next week. They've been frequent and very welcome visitors over the years. During our times together, we engage in the usual camp activities—swimming, canoeing, walking backwoods trails, reading and reminiscing. We also engage in a unique activity: Lake Dancing.

Lake Dancing is an improvisational activity, requiring an IPod (it used to be a CD player and before that a cassette player), some improvised instruments or props, and a good sized bottle of cheap red wine (CRW). Fortified by the CRW, we pick a song to play, gather our implements (instruments) and begin to dance and sing.

Here are some of our Lake Dances

Rake Dancing: you'll need a leaf rake, an Elvis collection that includes "Love Me Tender, "Don't be Cruel," "Hound Dog," and "Jail House Rock," and, of course, the CRW. The rake serves as a standup microphone which you grip and caress as you croon (groan is more like it) "Love Me Tender." Then you hand off the rake to the next person, who uses it as an air guitar for "Don't be Cruel." The third person vigorously claws the ground (this is an outside dance) with the rake, following the rhythm of "Jail House Rock" or "Hound Dog." You all take a break to sip some CRW, then start all over with new musicians.

Tong Dancing: You'll need at least a couple of pairs of the tongs used to grip fire logs, an ABBA collection, and more CRW. The tong holders clang their instruments together in concert with the syncopated rhythms of the ABBA song (it doesn't matter which one—they all sound pretty much the same) that's playing, and, if there are at least three dancers, you perform a chorus line dance. If you get really good at it, you can pass the jug of CRW along the line of tong musicians, and, if it's early in the evening, take a swig without missing a step or a clank.

Towel Dancing: This is best on rainy evenings just after dinner. Supplies include freshly washed, wet dishes, a number of dry towels and two dancers. Something like a Strauss waltz works well, as the dance involves a lot of swaying and graceful leg movement. The dishwasher hands the plate to the first dancer with a flourish; the first dryer wipes one side of the plate, gracefully passes it with one hand between his gracefully moving legs, grabs it with the other hand and gracefully hands it off to the drying partner, who finishes the job and with a pirouette puts it in the cupboard. The CRW is only passed around after the last dish has been safely shelved.

This year, we've been talking about inventing a new Lake Dance—something much less vigorous—after all, we aren't the kids we once were (or thought we were). One suggestion was a table dance, where we'd sit at the table, tap our feet, clap our hands, and slide the bottle of CRW across the table to each other, all the while playing a download of a Mantovani record.

After much discussion, we've decided that table dancing would require too much activity. So, we're just going to sit at the table, listen to Mantovani, slide the CRW bottle to each other, and boast about what wonderful Lake Dancers we once were.

3   Avian Encounters

One of the pleasures of summer is watching the birds of the lake and the woods, from the tiny hummingbird to the enormous bald eagle. Early in the season, transient birds stay overnight on their way north. Soon after, the permanent summer residents arrive. Many weeks later, when the loon chicks have learned to dive, when the hummingbird has relaxed his territorial aggressiveness, and when the transients reappear as they flee winter's approach, we know that another summer is nearing its conclusion.

The First Visitor

Here at the lake, there's a certain etiquette about visiting. When someone first arrives, people don't rush over to see them. The newcomers are given a chance to unpack, relax, and, after a long drive (anywhere from eight hours to four days), get their land legs. When we see them down at their dock, we wave, say "welcome back," and wait for a day or so before sauntering over to exchange family news and gossip from the long winter away from the lake. However, there's one neighbor who doesn't observe this polite behavior. As soon as we take down the protective shutters from the screen porch, he's right there.

He's the "chupacholo."

You may not have heard the term before; it's our family's corruption of the word "chuparosa," a Mexican term for "hummingbird," one who sucks on roses. (Actually they have very long tongues with which they lap up nectar and sugared water.) Through a series of permutations, the syllable "rosa" was replaced by "cholo," which is New Mexico slang for a young punk with an attitude. And the one at our lake certainly is a cholo. When he isn't gorging at the feeder, he

Fig. 3-1: Ruby-throated Hummingbird

perches on a tiny tree branch waiting to pick a fight with any other hummingbirds who dare to venture near.

For a couple of days after I'd arrived this year, I didn't have time to put up the feeder. He'd appear every hour or so, hover near the screen, and then depart. I don't know how to read the facial expressions of chupacholos, but I imagine his was one of disgust and annoyance at my tardiness. Now that the feeder is up, he appears every few minutes, and, when he's not chupa-ing, he's on guard, ready to assume his cholo role when an interloper shows up.

I was so glad when he first appeared this year. I'd been reading about how climate change was having devastating effects on migrating hummingbirds. It seems that flowers are blooming earlier along their migratory routes, and when the tiny travelers arrive at certain stopping points, their sources of nourishment have already bloomed and faded. For another year at least, my chupacholo has made it safely back to Crooked Lake.

He's not the most friendly of neighbors, and he's a bit of a mooch. But I hope that I'll have him/her (or his/her offspring) as my first visitor for many years to come.

Good-bye to a Good Neighbor

I'd been at the lake for a few days when I realized that I hadn't seen my nearest neighbor. He'd always been there when I arrived, be it mid-May, June, or early July. And he was always there when I left after Labor Day.

He was more a tenant than a neighbor, living in the vent near the peak of the front wall of the cabin. He'd leave for work just around sundown and I'd see his silhouette as he dipped and swooped back and forth between the cabin and the lake, harvesting his dinner of mosquitoes and moths.

We didn't interact much. I'd say hello when I first arrived and, when I closed up for the season, I'd call up goodbye to the vent. He stayed in his world and I stayed in mine.

He only came inside once. That was 14 or 15 years ago, when he must have been pretty young. (I like to think it's the same bat every year – it gives a sense of continuity.) I'd arrived at the lake when it was dark and the doors were open as I made several trips between the car and the house. I not only brought my stuff in, but a lot of mosquitoes as well.

The next morning, just at dawn, I heard a swooshing over my head as I lay in bed. I knew exactly what the sound was and I ducked under the covers. My tenant had come in after the mosquitoes last night. No wonder I'd fallen to sleep so easily—I hadn't heard any whining noises around my ears. The bat was doing its job.

I had to get up; I couldn't stay in bed all day. There was a lot of work to do. So, I put on my Tigers baseball cap and a thick jacket. I didn't want to find out whether or not the folklore about bats getting tangled in people's hair or being vampires was true. Waving a broom, I ushered him into the entry hall, opened the back door, letting in hordes of mosquitoes, and rushed back to the bedroom, slamming the door.

I ventured into the hall half an hour later; he was gone. After I'd closed the door, I rushed to get some mosquito lotion. That evening, I made sure I closed the outside doors, and I went to sleep without a buzz in my ears. I wasn't awakened the next dawn by swooshing noises.

We haven't been up close and personal since.

But this year, our bat isn't here. I don't know where he's gone. Has he found lodgings more to his liking? Has he met the love of his life and moved to another lake to be with her? I'll be hurt if he has, but happy for him.

Unfortunately, I think he's probably fallen victim to white nose syndrome, the disease that's already killed millions of his species.

Good-bye, little brown bat. I miss you.

Loons

It's an occasion of great joy when we see, or our neighbors tell us that they've seen the loons. Once threatened, the magnificent diving birds are making a comeback. We refer to them a THE loons, not some loons, as if they are old friends who've survived another winter and are here to share summer with us. They probably are the same birds we said good-bye to last fall. Barring death, the same pair will return to the same lake year after year. It's not an assured event. There are only two thousand pairs of nesting loons in all of Michigan. If someone disturbs their nest, both the mother and father will abandon it, meaning that there will be no baby loons for that season.

Fig. 3-2: The Common Loon

Two days ago, I heard the ululating sounds of loons and rushed down to the lake. There were two of the birds flying in great circles, each emitting cries. One seemed to be chasing the other. That evening, there was one loon fishing a couple of hundred feet from the end of the dock.

Puzzled, I contacted Scot, who writes a weekly bird column for the *Mining Journal*. He replied that what I'd first seen was probably a chase. The lake's resident male was defending his territory against an invader. That evening he was fishing, while his mate was in all likelihood incubating eggs.

And so, there are two more events to look forward to in the coming weeks: first, the mother taking her children for a cruise around the lake with them clinging to her back; then, a few weeks later, mother and father giving the growing children diving lessons.

A couple of weeks after the resident male loon had driven off the interloper, we were all delighted to see the two parents swimming in mid-lake with the offspring between them. All looked well.

But a week later, they swam with only one chick. Brian, who lives up the lake, said he had seen one of the little ones go under twice. "At first, I thought it was learning to dive," he reported. "But when it didn't come up the second time, I realized that it must have been eaten by a pike or a snapping turtle."

The parents continued their duties, circling the lake with the small survivor close behind them, one of them demonstrating diving while the other "stood" guard.

Then, one night, we heard a cacophony of loon cries: wailing and shrill warning shrieks. These went on for a good half hour. The next day, only one adult and one child swam on the lake. As they reached the bay opposite our dock, another adult flew in from the tree line and landed close to them. It stayed only a minute or two before retreating several hundred yards. Looking through the binoculars, I saw that the baby had jumped on its mother's back. No doubt the interloper had been rejected. At least that's what we wanted to believe.

Now, we hope that the parent and child will remain safe and that the child will continue to grow and learn survival skills. We want to see the loons next year.

Loons and Hope

Long ago, when I was in elementary school, we were shown a short movie called "The Loon's Necklace." Based on a Native legend, it told of how a loon had cured a human being of blindness. Years later, I learned that for many Native peoples, loons were symbols of healing and regeneration and were the totemic bird of shamans, traditional healers. I thought about these associations this morning.

Last night, I drove from the Marquette airport back to the lake under a full moon and remembered the solstice moon I'd paddled beneath just a month earlier and the loon who had accompanied me on my dawn excursion.

Then I thought about the terrible events that had occurred around the world since that last dawn, many of them while I was back in Albuquerque. Nice, Dallas, Baton Rouge, St. Paul, St. Joseph, Ankara—locations of a shattering violence that was so different from the calm, restfulness of the lake to which I was returning.

I thought about the news programs I'd watched in airports just a few hours ago and realized that words like "unification," "peace," "healing," and "dialogue" had been replaced by words of rudeness, vitriol and anger used in divisive, hateful monologues spoken by individuals of many different political persuasions.

And I felt sadness and a feeling of helplessness.

That night, the quietness of the lake was broken by a loon offering a full repertoire of sounds—ululations, shrieks of warning, calls of greeting. I wondered what had transpired in its life since our solstice encounter.

The next morning, when I walked down to the lake, I found out. There on the calm surface floated two adult loons and their two chicks. It hadn't been a lonely loon—a rejected suitor or grieving widow—that I'd heard last night, but one of a pair, fishing while the other tended the nest. The human world had been marked by violence and divisiveness; here four creatures of nature were living together in the way that loons have for centuries.

Although their world included natural predators, human invasion, and man-made pollution, the adults were preparing their offspring for a future.

I remembered Thomas Hardy's poem "In Time of the Breaking of Nations," written in 1916, when the world was being torn apart by what some people of that time called "the war to end all wars." Hardy noted that the simple, natural aspects of life continued and remarked: "This will go onward the same, though dynasties pass."

As the four loons swam away from me, the chicks moving toward their future, I felt a renewal of hope.

Duck! Ducks!

Before we came to the lake a couple of years ago, we spent a rainy spring afternoon sorting through a big box of photographs, separating the ones that were about the lake and putting them in a smaller box. We had intended to make them into a memory album to share with our visitors to the cabin, but they're still in the smaller box.

We paused over one of the pictures: Clare was sitting on the dock and sleeping around her were three or four mallard ducklings. The mother kept watch a few feet away. We had been warned that their poop could give us swimmer's itch if we continued to entice them to visit us by offering stale bread crusts. But we continued our offerings: they were entertaining company, and we didn't get swimmer's itch.

"You know," I said to her, "we haven't seen any ducks on the lake for a few years." We put the photograph in the smaller box and agreed that we missed the mallards. We started reminiscing about them as if they were dearly departed friends.

"Do you remember our first summer when we didn't have a dock? We used to sit on the bank and throw bread into the water when they arrived," Clare remarked. "One day, we decided to throw the bread on the ground. Finally one of them hopped out of the water, gobbled the bread and then glared at us. The rest of them followed."

"A few weeks later," I said, continuing the story, "we weren't outside when they arrived and one of them started waddling up the path to the cabin. I threw some bread out the door and started a bad habit. The mooches kept coming to the door, quacking rudely."

"Then there was the time we were all sitting on the bank. The ducklings were getting bigger then. One walked right past us and up the path. When nobody came to the door, he decided to fly back to the lake, but he had trouble getting off the ground," Clare laughed. "If I hadn't yelled, 'Duck!,' he'd have crashed into us!"

A couple of years later, when "our ducks" realized that they were "our ducks," we were able to entice them up onto the dock. After they'd duck-dived and bobbed up like little corks, they came for their treat, which we showed them and put on one of the steps to the dock. They got the idea, would come up for a snack, let Clare gently stroke them, and then arrange themselves around her for a post-prandial nap.

Ducklings pretty much look the same until they start growing their gender-specific feathers. But over the years, we noticed two that were distinct, and we gave them names. One we called "Sister," and a few weeks later our guess turned out to be right. Another, playing on the name of a character in the movie "Sixteen Candles," we called "Lame Duck Dong." He was a sad case. He was lame and had difficulty hopping up onto the dock. Moreover, he was shunned by his brothers and sisters. As the summer went on, he took to sitting alone on the neighbors' dock. Feeling sorry for him, I'd walk over and put some crusts a few feet away from him.

One summer, there were two families on the lake. We tried not to play favorites, and usually that worked, because only one flock would arrive at a time. But once, they both showed up simultaneously and, when I made a noise that was supposed to sound like "quack," but actually sounded like I was clearing my throat, the two flocks swam toward the dock, each coming from different directions, the mothers leading the way. When they spotted each other, the mothers squawked angrily, reared into the air beating their feathers, and then charged at each other, heads down, and began battering one another. I yelled loudly and they all took off. It was later in the summer and we didn't have a mallard visitor for the rest of our stay.

There have been sad moments in our relationships. At least once a year, the flock would arrive missing a member. And one time, as they were swimming through a bunch of reeds, there was a splashing and great row. One of the babies went under and never came up.

There is still much to engage us as we sit at the dock: watching the bald eagle ride the air currents far above us, seeing a little turtle head bob up in the water and then disappear, hearing the raucous cry of the kingfisher as he flies from a tree, dives into the water and emerges with dinner in his beak.

But I miss our friendship with the ducks. I wish they'd come back, even if they gave us swimmer's itch.

A Solitary Visitor

Since Clare and Alberto left for the city yesterday morning, it's been quite quiet at this end of the lake. None of the nearby cabins are occupied. No one has raced down the back road on a motorized toy, and the pontoon boats have stayed in the middle of the lake.

Then, this afternoon, I had a visitor. A great blue heron landed on our dock, the first one I'd seen at the lake for a couple of years. I stayed inside, let the sleeping dogs lie, and moved slowly and quietly to the screened porch to gaze at it.

It stood on the dock for well over an hour. At first it hunched down, neck bent into an "S," no doubt resting from its flight (from wherever that was). Then it "stood up," craning its neck to look out at the lake, occasionally taking a step one way or the other, and once going down one of the steps that leads from the dock to the water.

As I watched, I heard the clunking of an awkwardly paddled kayak approaching. A young girl came close to the dock to get a closer look at my visitor. She called back down the lake saying she'd found this strange big bird. Herons are solitary creatures; they don't like human beings getting into their space. Even if they get to know you and are used to your presence, they will only stand your being around if you keep your distance. It resented the intrusion, unfolded its wings, and launched itself into the air.

"Good-bye," I said softly, as it sailed majestically into the distance. "Thanks for dropping by." The kayaker did a U-turn and disappeared around the point.

I returned to my tasks at the computer, but found my mind wandering from the tedious work of creating an index for a book about beer to questions about the bird on the dock. "Where did it come from? Would it become a resident of the lake? Why had it decided to land and then stand for so long on my dock? Had the kayaker's intrusion scared it off for good?" I was sorry the girl had come so close and felt a little sad at its departure.

I googled "herons," "symbolism," and "folklore" and discovered that these loners, these solitary "fishermen," have many meanings and have many stories told about them in cultures from around the world. Among the words frequently applied to them are "wisdom," "judgment," "determination," "self-reliance," and "patience." They are associated with tranquility and stillness. That was my visitor, and before the interruption, his presence had filled me with a sense of tranquility.

I read a few folktales about cranes and then remembered a piece of local Crooked Lake folklore. Next to the patient, determined great blue heron and others of his tribe, the best fisherman on the lake had been Bill, who for several years had been my neighbor a few cabins to the north. He was pretty good and used to supply nearly all the fish that his church used in their annual charity dinner. Some of the locals used to say that the fishing had become so poor because he'd caught nearly every fish in the lake.

But, one day Bill got his comeuppance. He'd been fishing on the far side of the lake and, not far away, so was a heron. They were biting pretty good that day and, after he'd landed a dozen or so, Bill motored back to his dock and dumped his catch in the submerged wire cage to keep them fresh until he was ready to clean them.

When he returned to the other side of the lake, he noticed that the heron had disappeared. Then he heard a lot of splashing around his dock. There, standing next to the wire cage was the heron, picking off the trapped fish at his leisure.

About an hour after the young girl had driven my guest off, I looked up from my desk and out the window. The heron had come back, and this time it had hopped up on one of the benches on the dock.

I felt honored.

Cry of the Heron

During the summers, when many out-of-town guests arrived at his family home in Victoria, my father would "camp out" in the boathouse at the bottom of the lot. He loved it, except for one evening. Here's how, many years later, he described the experience:

I'd been reading Sherlock Holmes and had scared my way through one of the more frightening epics. In the story a harsh supernatural sound from a desolate bit of country provided the appropriate background for Conan Doyle's web of mystery. I'd retire alone to the boathouse at 9:30 and by 10 I'd be asleep. At 10.15, I'd be awake listening in the dark to the eeriest sound that ever struck human ears. It was a grating squawk, the despairing cry of a lost soul, only it was real.

The hair on my back stood up so stiffly, it practically forced me into a sitting position. When it had been repeated three nights, I found the desperate courage that's born of fear, and stayed up to investigate. At 10:15 the cry came to me from the sky. Against the uncertain light of stars, I saw a shape sailing from the hill toward the sea.

Fig. 3-3: The Great Blue Heron takes flight

By discreet daylight inquiry, I learned that it was a blue heron, gliding down to roost in the kelp bed at the mouth of the bay. Once it was identified, the eeriness went out of the big bird's cry. It became familiar. I'd lie awake to hear it just to make sure it was bedding down safely for the night. The big wader never knew it, but we became pretty good friends in a remote sort of way.

Victoria Daily Times, May 14, 1954

"I Heerd Feetprints"

Last night, I thought of a column my father wrote about an old family story. It concerned one of my aunts when she was a child. She'd been sleeping on the porch of the family's lakeside cabin when she came in wide-eyed and, her voice trembling, announced to the adults who were sitting reading by the light of the Coleman lantern hanging above the kitchen table: "I heerd feetprints by the porch!"

Last night, I heerd feetprints and I, too, was alarmed. When I took the dogs out for their last sniff-around, sounds like small-dogs yapping or ducks squawking came from the north. Fearing there might be coyotes, I quickly called Hankie and Trina inside and went to bed.

As I lay there, the noises seemed to be getting closer and louder. In addition to the yipping and squawking, a groaning noise came through the trees. The sounds came closer and closer. Suddenly, they were right outside my window.

Had one of my neighbors succumbed to cabin fever and begun wandering dementedly through the woods? Or, worse still, was a Windigo, a cannibalistic monster that roamed the north woods, moaning as it searched for victims, about to break through the window and devour me, Trina, and Hankie, who was trembling as he pressed close to me?

I jumped from bed and ran around the house, locking the windows and doors and turning all the inside and outside lights on. Then breathless, I grabbed a miniature baseball bat off the souvenir shelf and sank into my creaky recliner-rocker.

Seeking to calm myself, I picked up my copy of *Birds of Michigan* which was on the side table. On page 150, I read these words: "sounds like a dog barking just before giving an eight-hoot howl..." The "feetprints I heerd" were those of a barred owl.

I put my mini-bat back on the shelf, turned out all the lights, opened the bedroom window, climbed into bed, and went to sleep.

Up with the Birds... Sort Of

When we're at the lake we retire shortly after sunset and arise early. We're healthy, although not so wealthy or wise. Usually, we leave the dock when the gulls have departed for their rookery and, although we don't rise with the birds, we do enjoy listening to the myriad aubades as we lie in bed gathering our wits about us.

It hasn't always been this way.

A few decades ago, just as we were drifting off, we'd frequently be startled into complete wakefulness by the three-note call of a whippoorwill. It wasn't a gentle nighttime lullaby. It was very loud, and it was repeated and repeated and repeated. From what we could gather, it was carrying on a conversation with another whippoorwill across the lake, because when our bird took a breath, a similar three-note reply came from afar.

This went on for three or four weeks. We're not sure whether "our" whippoorwill was warning its cross-lake interlocutor to stay on its side of the water or inviting it to come over for a visit, or just announcing to it that in the house beside the tree were human beings who went to bed far too early. If this were the case, it didn't cause us to change our habits. Then, one day, it moved down the lake and its conversations no longer disturbed our early-to-bed routine.

One spring, our early-to-rise routine arrived too early. A couple of times a week, I'd been travelling two hours each way to Sault Ste. Marie to teach a night class. I'd return home around midnight and have a snack before bed. Thursday night was special—I didn't have to worry about being early-to-rise the next day. There were no papers to grade or classes to prepare until Monday. I'd have a beer with my snack and retire looking forward to a Friday morning sleep-in.

But the local woodpecker had other ideas. Every Friday, and it seemed to be only on Friday, he'd arrive on my roof at sunrise and decide that I was a slug-a-bed whose time for sleeping was over. He'd stand beside the sheet-metal stove pipe and begin to noisily tap out some kind of avian Morse code on the metal: rat-a-tat-tat, five or six times in a row. Then a pause. I'd start to drift off and he'd start again. A few weeks later, I told a friend about these rude awakenings. He suggested that the bird was cleaning or sharpening its bill, I don't recall which. But I think it was pure orneriness, a kind of "if I have to be up at this time, you should be too" attitude.

I still hear woodpeckers around the cabin, but now they're working on trees, not stove pipes. I haven't heard any whippoorwills for many, many years. When I checked on this with the people who know, I found out that across the northern Midwest as well as other parts of the continent, the population of whippoorwills had dropped drastically since the turn of the century. They hadn't earned the label "endangered" yet, but they were in dire straits. The causes were man-made. Pesticides had drastically lessened the numbers of insects that formed their major food source, and land clearing had caused serious habitat loss. I wasn't hearing them as I tried to drift off to sleep because there weren't any of them around to keep me awake.

I'm not upset that the woodpecker has taken its "rat-a-tat-tat" elsewhere. But I am saddened to hear of the plight of the whippoorwills. If I were once again to have my early-to-bed routine disturbed by a very loud three-note call followed by one from across the lake, I wouldn't be annoyed. I would be happy to think that one of the lake's former avian residents was making a comeback.

4   **The Great Indoors**

Part of the great charm of having our Little Cabin in the Big Woods is not just spending as much time as possible at the shore, on the lake , and in the woods, but also enjoying time indoors. Over the years, the house has developed its own character. It is cozy and comfortable, and when the north winds blow and the rain forms large pools in the driveway out back, it is fun to fuss with the fireplace and then to watch the dance of the flames behind the plate glass window, to smell the delicious aromas of dinner simmering on the stove, and to settle comfortably into the recliner-rocker that, over the years, has become almost form-fitting and read a book, or, warm and comfortable, lookout at the nasty weather raging outside.

A Retirement Home

"So you've bought a retirement home," a friend remarked when, many decades ago, I told him we'd purchased our Little Cabin in the Big Woods.

"Oh, no!" I replied. "It's not insulated and it's totally inaccessible for five months in the winter. And besides, I don't intend to retire for another fifteen years." (It turned out to be twenty-five).

"I'm not talking about you!" he responded with a chuckle. "I'm talking about old appliances, sagging mattresses, and chipped dinner-ware. When people with country places buy new stuff for their city homes, the old things usually spend several years of retirement at the cabin."

Looking back, I realize that we had, indeed, purchased a retirement cabin. It was small—22 feet by 24—with no indoor plumbing. There was a pitcher pump for water and a big pot to warm it on the stove.

There was a narrow path through the birches to a little building that had a door with a half moon cut out near the top.

We did have electricity, with an old-fashioned fuse box and a little package of fuses on top of it. "Don't stand between it and the pump if there's an electrical storm," the man we bought the place from warned. "Once a lightning strike jumped from the box and knocked my wife down." The fridge had a rounded top and little freezer compartment that could hold one ice cube tray, a package of meat, a canister of frozen juice and a very small brick of ice cream. The gas stove was lit by match. Both had been in their retirement home for many years.

The dishware that came with the place must have been a wedding present long ago. There were ornate paintings on the chipped plates; the serving dish with handles had a crack through it. Most of the glasses had started their lives as jelly jars with rounded lips around the top that made them suitable for drinking out of. A couple of the pots had corks screwed onto their lids.

The table was an old card table and around it were four chairs that must once have been part of a dinette suite. The bed in the foldout couch was lumpy and showed signs of having been the occasional winter residence of small creatures. The recliner no longer reclined.

Still, we were delighted to be there in our very own Little Cabin in the Big Woods.

But after a year or two, some changes were made, and the cabin became less of a retirement home. First, the fridge began freezing the lettuce in the bottom compartment and melting the ice cubes in the top one. Lighting the oven became an adventure. In fact, one time, so much gas accumulated that the door of the warming compartment blew open. The pump stopped working one August when the lake levels were very low. When we opened up one season, the mice had violated their winter lease agreement and fled as we opened the door. They hadn't tidied up after themselves.

Then there was the summer when it rained nearly every day for a week. The mosquitoes loved it, but it sure made the walk along the tree-lined path mighty unpleasant, particularly at night. The cabin became damp and the picturesque looking Franklin-type stove proved to be better at belching smoke than driving out the dampness. That was when Carol and Clare decided that the cabin could no longer be a retirement home.

And so, over a handful of seasons, we replaced the stove and the fridge. The ice cubes froze and starting the oven to bake a blueberry pie was no longer a perilous activity. I bought a reconditioned recliner that reclined (for a few years). We replaced the plates, bowls, and mugs with ones we could put in the microwave. Most important, we built an addition so that, as the song from "Oklahoma" says, we could walk to privies in the rain and never wet our feet. We bought a wonderful wood-burning heater with a glass front so that we could watch the flames and avoid the smoke.

I felt a little guilty in later years when we added a couple of new-fangled inventions: internet and a satellite dish. But I argued that, if I were to be spending extended summers there and doing a lot of writing, they were necessities.

It's been nearly forty years since we bought our retirement home and began changing its status. But now, when I look over some of the "improvements" made over many summers, I'm beginning to see that many things are reaching their retirement age. Do we need to buy another cabin to move them to?

Bookcases

When we first bought the Little Cabin in the Big Woods, we inherited a small, three-shelf bookcase. On the top shelf were some cones from the big white pine just outside by the back door and a conch shell that certainly wasn't from our lake. The cones had had been decorated with sparkle-paint. There were a some books on the lower two shelves: a few Harlequin romances, a six-gun's worth of westerns, a long-outdated AAA tour book for Indiana and Ohio, and a copy of one of the great 20th century children's classics, *The Little House on the Prairie.*

By the end of our first summer, we'd added a lot more books. Many are still identifiable by the rusty water stains at the bottom of the pages. They're the ones that Clare, Carol, and some of our friends read on the dock. After cooling off in the lake, they'd sit deck chairs, resting the books on their wet bathing suits. We also added many nature guides: the Peterson bird books, books about flowers, and trees, and animal tracks.

By the time we left at the end of August, it was apparent we needed another bookcase. Now, close to four decades later, we have five. There are more of the rust-colored, wrinkled read-on-the-dock books,

books we'd brought from home, and a growing number of books we've bought at Marquette's Snowbound Books. It's a place you can't leave empty handed.

Many of the books on our shelves are cookbooks, forgotten or hard-to-find classics that Carol and Clare read with delight and used to guide their preparation of delicious meals. Others are books I've binge read over the years: the Harry Potter series; Tony Hillerman's Navajo detective stories; Isabel Allende's South America novels. I've also got copies of Thoreau's *Walden*, Aldo Leopold's *A Sand County* Almanac, and *Selected Poems of Robert Frost*. I read in each of them regularly, delighting in their responses to the natural worlds they celebrate.

Until 2014, it was a pretty eclectic mix of books, very randomly shelved.

That's when I purchased my fifth bookcase. During the winter, I'd been collecting stories about the legendary logger Paul Bunyan to use as background material for my own retellings. I wanted to keep them close to the writing table/computer desk in the office/storeroom and the other bookcases were too full to move.

Bookcase number five has become home to my Upper Peninsula collection. There are probably close to a hundred titles tightly packed onto the three shelves. The top one contains the Paul Bunyan volumes, along with other folktale books. My favorites are Harold Fenton's *Legends of Paul Bunyan*, a collection by several authors which shows that there are as many Pauls as there are retellers; Richard M. Dorson's *Bloodstoppers and Bearwalkers: Folk Traditions of the Upper Peninsula,* a gathering of stories from the various cultural groups that have called the UP home; and *Schoolcraft's Indian Legends*, a white man's retelling of the life and deeds of Nanabozho, the culture hero of the Anishinaabe (Ojibway/Chippewa) people. It's an interesting and rather biased adaptation that served as the source for Longfellow's *Song of Hiawatha.*

The middle shelf includes histories, new and old, of the Upper Peninsula, along with a number of guide books. Russell M. Magnaghi has covered the many eras and many topics of the area's history in *Upper Peninsula of Michigan: a History.* Lewis C. Reimann, in *Incredible Seney,* presents a great portrait of the logging era's most notorious "hell town in the pines." *Michigan's Upper Peninsula Almanac,* by Ron Jolly and Karl Bohnak, makes for wonderful casual browsing: it's full of facts and figures of just about everything and everywhere in the UP.

The bottom shelf is my favorite: novels and stories about the U.P. Most of the shelf is occupied by the works of Jim Harrison, who had a cabin near Grand Marais for a couple of decades late in the last century. My favorite novels are written about the country north of Seney, an area that gained literary notoriety when Ernest Hemingway's story "The Big Two-Hearted River" was published shortly after World War One. I'm particularly partial to Harrison's *Brown Dog,* a collection of novellas, some of them set in the area south of the Pictured Rocks, about the misadventures of the title hero. Ellen Airgood's *South of Superior* is a novel from the Grand Marais area in which the heroine comes to live for the first time in the old family stomping grounds.

The other day, I realized that bookcase number five had become overfull. I'm planning a trip to Snowbound Books in a couple of days. So, tomorrow, I'm stopping in at the local furniture store to pickup bookcase number six.

Television at the Lake

Long ago, when you could count the number of TV stations on your thumbs, my grandmother decided to buy a used television for the lake. One evening we gathered to watch "The Untouchables." At the story's climax, Eliot Ness's crew set fire to kegs of whiskey. As the flames flickered on the 12 inch black and white screen, smoke started rising from the back of the set. The next day, my grandmother bought a brand new set.

Three or four decades later, we had a similar experience at the Little Cabin in the Big Woods. When we bought the place we had decided to enjoy pure nature. We installed a phone, but agreed not to have a television set. However, early during our second summer in the UP, after four straight days of rain, we abandoned our resolution, made a trip to Marquette and picked up a 12 inch set.

That night, we watched a baseball game. In the seventh inning, the Tigers got really hot, overcoming an eight-run deficit. They were so hot that, just after they'd scored the go-ahead run, smoke rose from the back of our set. The next day, we were back in Marquette.

One time, before the leaves had fully opened up, I was twisting the dial on the TV when I noticed a faint image on a channel that had always been blank. I was surprised to hear the newscasters speaking in southern, rather than Yooper accents. Then a commercial came on for a car dealership in Baton Rouge, Louisiana, from where the broadcast was coming. A few days later, the rotting pole to which our battered aerial was attached blew over and we spent the rest of the summer with only one channel available. It was from Green Bay—and I learned more about the Packers than I ever needed to know.

Many years later, when I had retired and began to spend extended summers at the lake and when we'd moved into the 100 plus channel universe, I bought a bigger television (with a remote control) and installed a satellite dish. I watched the hockey finals, Tiger baseball, the *PBS News Hour*, and some favorites on Turner Classic Movies, but not much else. Occasionally, when it was rainy and I was bored, I'd waste 15 minutes clicking through all the channels and finding nothing of interest turn the set off.

I still have that TV and another one, a high-definition set with an enormous screen. It only gets one channel—the Crooked Lake Nature Channel. The colors are wonderful and constantly changing. When the north wind blows and the trees sway, the whitecaps race to the south. There's lots of action: a squirrel scampers along the bank, pontoon boats chug slowly by, loons disappear under water and reappear where you'd least expect. If you watch early in the morning, you can see deer stepping daintily and cautiously as they head to the shore for their daily drink. And in the evenings, the sunsets are gorgeous and different each day. Every once in a while, a two-legged intruder walks across the screen.

My big screen, high-definition TV is not a well-known brand. But I wouldn't trade it for anything. And the programming doesn't cost over a hundred bucks a month, with a minimum six month contract for each year.

It's called "My Front Window."

The Joys of a Fireplace

Last night, the temperature dropped below 50 degrees for the first time in a couple of weeks. In anticipation of a chilly morning, I'd chopped extra kindling and tied knots in rolled pages of yesterday's *Mining Journal*. When I walked into the front room just after sunrise, I could see fog rising from the lake.

Our airtight wood burner with the window in front that I call our third TV needed coaxing this morning and I was glad that I'd rolled up all of the newspaper. After I'd made a good bed of coals with the kindling, I added some smaller pieces of split birch, poured myself a cup of coffee and sat in the old rocker recliner. My gaze shifted between the flames licking the birch and the rays of sunlight beginning to shine through the trees.

I thought about the first time the former owner of the cabin had shown us the place. We were delighted with the Franklin-type stove in the corner. "It works really well—draws wonderfully," he enthusiastically explained. It didn't. The pipes had four elbows before it met the roof. Unless you constantly fed it very small pieces of very dry wood, smoke began to curl from the top of the opening. Luckily, there was a small propane heater and so we very seldom used the Franklin-style stove. But we missed the flames and when Norm and his crew were doing some renovations, we had him install the one we now have.

The fire was beginning to die down, so I added some more birch and poured myself a second cup of coffee. My mind again wandered into the past, and I remembered the fireplace in the cabin of my childhood summers. Like his father, my father believed that a house without a fireplace was not a home, even if the house was a two-room, uninsulated shack in the quite dark and generally relatively damp woods. We had a wood stove that usually kept one of the rooms warm; but, my father lamented, you couldn't watch the flames or fuss with the logs to get them burning just the right way.

So, when I was about seven-years-old, he decided that he would build a fireplace at the lake. He got some plans from the library, advice from an acquaintance who had built his own fireplace, and bricks from a recently demolished building in town. Over many, many weekends, he loaded the trunk of the car with them, while my two sisters and I sat in the back seat, wedged in between the duffel bag of clothes and the box of groceries. When we arrived at the lake, it was the duties of the three of us to pack the duffel bag, box of groceries, and the bricks—two or three at a time—down to the cabin.

On spring weekends and during summer vacation, the fireplace took shape and the chimney rose above the roofline. The facing around the opening was made with cobblestones we all harvested from a nearby creek. In early fall, we had our first fire. Our dinner was hot dogs roasted on long sticks we'd cut from a sapling nearby and then marshmallows, black on the outside and still cold on the inside.

The fireplace was my father's pride and joy. In his newspaper columns he often wrote about sitting beside it, looking into the flames and thinking about the gems of wisdom in his favorite poem, "The Rubaiyat of Omar Khayyam." The last time I visited him, just a few months before his death, it was a cold, damp March day. That evening, we sat in front of the fire, sipping brandy and reminiscing.

Back in the present, I noticed that the room was getting very hot, so hot that I opened a couple of windows. By this time, the sun had burned away the mist on the lake and rays were shining in the side windows. I let the fire die, finished my coffee, made breakfast and then headed outside to do the morning chores. It was still brisk outside, so I warmed myself up by chopping more kindling and splitting some birch logs. When it got cold again, I'd need the wood for a fire that would drive out the chill and rekindle more memories.

A Shelf of Memories

Over the last few days, I've been worried about the occasional mouse tracks I've been finding all around the cabin. So, armed with rolls of paper towels and a very large can of disinfectant spray, I've been on a cleaning campaign.

In most spots, the job was fairly quick and easy—spray, wipe and move on. But there's one place where I lingered, the shelf on which, over the years, we've put the little trinkets and mementoes people have brought us. The cleaning took only a few minutes, the putting things back on the shelf, a long time. I would pick up each item, gaze at it, and think of the people who gave the gift and what it meant, then and now.

First was a little matchbox motor home. One year, when we came to camp at Colwell Lake, we rented a motor home from someone in Marquette. Craig and Jan, who had joined Carol, Clare, and me, brought the little toy as a joke gift. "We know you've always wanted one of these, so here you are," they told us. As it was, that summer they'd helped us discover the cabin. We forgot all our dreams of a motor home, but we never forgot the fun we had the time we stayed in that one, which was nearing the end of a very long life of very poor treatment. The tiny replica was the first souvenir to be placed on the shelf of our new summer home.

Fig. 4-1: The Shelf: matchbox motorhome at right

Next, I picked up a plush loon. Clare had bought it one year when there were no loons on the lake. We had missed the nighttime sounds of the birds and their daytime diving and needed something to remind us of what had been an essential part of summers past. I squeezed it and it still worked, giving out a long, mournful cry.

Beside it was a tiny bell with a ribbon tie. It had been a place decoration at Diane's wedding. She, along with her parents, had visited us when we first bought the cabin. Its clapper still works. I shook it and it made a tiny tinkle. I thought of the rainy day when we'd all sat in the newly-purchased cabin, everyone offering ideas of how to get the smoky fireplace to work properly. None of the suggestions worked.

There's a little plastic green whistle that was a prize in one of the crackers that had been part of the festivities in a Christmas-in-July celebration. It may have been with Craig and Jan or Bruce and Phyllis—I don't remember. I know Deb was a regular guest. I blew into it and it emitted a squawk that probably sounded better than the male chorus that, later that night, tried to sing "Silent Night" while sipping a little too much brandy.

Next came two very small statues: one of Paul Bunyan, the other of Babe the Blue Ox, who looked diminutive next to the legendary logger. I'd bought them at a gift store that was located beside an enormous statue of Paul and Babe. I'd been travelling through the UP visiting places that were associated with 19th century logging and that I wanted to use as settings for some of my retellings of the legends. I learned a great deal on the trip and remembered the kindness of the librarians, historical society presidents, and gift store owners who'd increased my knowledge, not only of the fictional character, but also of the lumber culture of long ago.

I arranged these and a few other less memorable keepsakes back on the shelf, leaving a space in the center for the most wonderful item of all. It was a life-sized carving of a daffodil, complete with a bug hole in one of the spears. Grace, one of the pioneers of Crooked Lake, had carved it in a craft class she was taking. She had brought it to the lake and presented it to Clare and me in memory of Carol, whom we had lost a few months earlier. Daffodils had been Carol's favorite flower. As I carefully placed it on the shelf, I felt a sweet melancholy.

In total, the monetary value of these souvenirs is not great. But value of the memories they evoke of wonderful people and happy times is inestimable.

The Lives of Clothes

A few years ago, when Clare and I were looking through an old box of photographs, we came across a picture of the family taken sometime in the late 1980s. "That shirt you're wearing in the picture—didn't you wear it at the cabin last summer?" she asked.

I probably had. When clothes become a little frayed at the collar, worn at the knees, button-challenged, or just plain out-of-style, they're usually good enough to wear in the woods. So off to the lake they go.

Today, wearing the shirt from the photo (it's got another year or two of use left), I decided to sort out my clothes closet. It was an historical experience.

One of the oldest articles was a timber cruiser's vest I used to wear when I worked in the summers for the British Columbia Forest Service in the late 1950s. It has great pockets to stuff mosquito lotion bottles and keys into and, when I ride out to the highway to the post box, pouches in which to put the mail and the *Mining Journal*. It's almost as old is a Black Watch tartan shirt my mother bought me in when I started college and that Clare wears on the dock on cold days.

The lives of blue jeans are also extended at the lake: frayed ones for hiking and chopping wood and worn at the knees ones for when I'm house painting (infrequently). When the tears become too big, I make them into cutoffs. I found three pair of these during my sorting. But, I'm going to have to get rid of two. I can't get them buttoned up.

On another stay-in-doors afternoon, I took inventory of the tee shirts spilling off a shelf, seeing which ones had more life in them and which deserved to go to their final resting place … the rag bag.

There were eighteen in all.

Four were plain ones in very good condition. I wouldn't be ashamed to wear any of them to town.

Another carried memories: a "This Old House" tee shirt we got for pledging to the local educational TV station. We all liked watching the show as a family—so it has a strong sentimental attachment. It's a keeper.

Four bore emblems of sports teams. Two of the teams are defunct: the Maui Stingrays and the Duluth-Superior Dukes. They could be conversation pieces if I wore them in the right places. The third is a new Seattle Seahawks tee shirt I brought out here to wear when the team is on TV. I'll have to make sure that there are no Green Bay fans around. The fourth celebrates the team I wrote program articles for a decade or more ago: the Edmonton Trappers. All of the shirts are in good shape—four more keepers.

There are two about drinking local Lake Superior area beers. I'm thinking of going to a beer festival in Marquette soon. I'll wear one then and the other next year.

Three are ones Clare designed for the University of Alberta Anthropology Club over a quarter of a century ago. They're pretty frayed at the collar, but far too important to let go.

Two have pictures of one of my dogs, Zoe, on them. Can't be washed, but have to be kept. She was a great pal.

Another has a saying about the UP and flatulence. I can wear it around my vulgar friends.

One is beyond repair. Its collar is in tatters; the armpits are yellowed and ripped; there are brown streaks of paint from a job I did sometime in the distant past. I threw it into the rag bag and put the other seventeen back on the shelf.

Storm Watching

It happens a few times each summer. You're inside finishing your coffee, cleaning up breakfast dishes, reading, or sitting at the table writing. The radio is on. Then a screech, like the sound of an old-fashioned claxon announcing the end of a quarter at a basketball game, interrupts the classical music.

After three or four blasts, a monotone, computerized voice delivers a message. A storm is striking a specified county a certain distance away. The direction that the storm is coming from, usually west or southwest, is stated. The robot voice tells us whether heavy rain, hail, lighting and damaging winds are parts of the offering. The calm, authoritative voice advises people in the path of the advancing storm seek shelter indoors.

You check that the windows are closed and walk down to the dock to make sure the canoe is securely tied and to bring the plastic chairs to the cleared space in front of the cabin. Then you go back to your desk, occasionally glancing out the window toward the west to see if anything is happening.

Usually, not much does happen. There are some whitecaps on the lake, a few small branches are blown off trees, and puddles form along the pathway. The clouds pass, the sun shines again, the whitecaps vanish.

But not during what those of us who were around at the time refer to as the big storm of "Oh-four" and still talk about. The usual caxton sounds and monotone warnings were given—but with an added caveat: winds could reach velocities of nearly 100 miles an hour. People were advised, not only to seek shelter indoors, but to stay away from windows. I took the usual precautions and then sat in my recliner a good ten feet away from the window. The lights flickered a couple of times and then went out. So I put my book down and looked out the window and across the lake.

First the gray clouds took on a strange, almost green luminescence. "It looked like an atomic bomb had gone off somewhere," a neighbor later remarked. The treetops on the near shore started swaying slightly in the breeze. Then the wind, which had been blowing from the north, suddenly shifted and blew directly from the west across the lake at the house. The whitecaps galloped toward the shore.

The rain came down in sheets, the shoreline disappeared, the chairs tumbled across the open space into the underbrush. Flashes of lightning, followed in decreasing numbers of seconds by ever louder thunder, illuminated the yard, now littered with branches.

It was a spectacular sight. I sat spellbound in my chair, while the dog tried to find protection on my lap.

Then the thumpings began: at first somewhere out in the front yard that I could no longer see, then beside the house. They became more frequent. My chair was right beneath a skylight, so I retreated to the kitchen and sat on the floor next to the cabinets. If a tree came through the roof, I'd at least have some protection. The dog wedged herself between me and the cupboards.

In half an hour, it was all over. The whitecaps had disappeared, the branches swayed relatively gently, the torrents had subsided to showers. I looked out the front window: the canoe was still there although almost submerged; the clearing was littered with branches, some of them pretty big; the plastic chairs were nowhere to be seen.

When I looked out the back window, I discovered what had caused all the thumping. The usual post-rain puddles in the driveway were ponds. At least a dozen trees and been blown down or were leaning dangerously. The power line running above the driveway hung precariously low. None of the trees had hit the car and the driveway was clear.

When I walked the shore trail later in the afternoon, I discovered others weren't so lucky. A great white pine had fallen across a boat trailer, bending it nearly double. Fortunately, the boat wasn't on the trailer; but it was completely submerged, motor and all, in the water. Another tree had fallen across power lines, pulling the metal mast attached to the wall of a cabin and most of the wall to the ground. Other places had suffered near misses.

Year later, a couple of us were reminiscing about the event. "That was a real humdinger," my neighbor said.

It sure was. I'm glad I'd obeyed the monotone voice's orders and taken shelter indoors and moved away from the windows.

That Lonely Whistle

Last night it was very quiet at the lake. None of the nearby camps had been opened; it was too early in the year for the evening chorus of frogs or whine of mosquitoes. There was a very slight breeze from the north, but it didn't rustle the leaves, since the trees were still in bud. Only the occasional hum of car tires from the highway a mile distant broke the silence.

As I sat in the dark on the screen porch, I heard a faint sound that I hadn't heard for many years. It was two whistle blasts of a train approaching the Shingleton crossing, ten miles distant, and was carried, no doubt, through the leafless forest by the northern zephyr. The sound took me in memory to my childhood in Western Canada and in imagination to the Upper Peninsula's logging era of the late 19th century.

At night, long ago, we'd hear the freight trains laboring up the steep grade of the Malahat Mountain and giving two short blasts of their steam whistles when they came to the crossing over the road leading to Shawnigan Lake. If we were down at the beach, we would see the light at the front of the locomotive shining through the trees across the lake.

In the 1950s, the steam locomotives were replaced by diesels whose churning motors and air horn blasts lacked the romance of the old trains. Now, with the Vancouver Island roads making truck transit so much easier, faster, and cheaper than rail, the old night freight trains have disappeared.

In Michigan in the late 19th century, as the timber stands near rivers were exhausted, logging moved inland. Hastily constructed railway lines, which were easily installed and later easily removed and relocated to other locations, sprung up throughout the UP. Flatbeds of logs were pulled by small Shea engines to Lake Superior or the main logging rivers to be floated or driven to the nearest sawmills.

A few years ago, Upper Peninsula historian James Carter created a map of the logging roads of the east-central UP. The railroad lines look like a network of nerves or arteries laid out upon the land. In many ways they were the arteries of the logging industry and, when the industry moved west, they remained only as roadbeds and rapidly overgrown right-of-ways.

The Shea engines played a role in the Paul Bunyan legends told by loggers in the19th century. It seems that Babe the Blue Ox, who was Bunyan's steadiest and most trustworthy worker, as well as his much spoiled and beloved pet, lost a contest with an engine. With the increase in the number of logging railroads in the area, Babe was becoming obsolete. He had set records for hauling the largest loads of logs along the icy roads. People used to come from miles around just to see the legendary creature. Paul had been so proud of him that the ox was given a special stall in the barn and fed stacks of pancakes doused with butter (a rare commodity) and syrup.

Babe was more than annoyed about the Shea engines taking over his job; he got downright ornery. He was in his stall one day, sulking, when he heard an engine chugging toward camp. He burst through the side of the barn, raced to the tracks, and planted his feet firmly on the ties. He'd settle this matter once and for all. The train came around the bend and Babe charged. He knocked the engine off the tracks, but he didn't survive the encounter. The legendary Blue Ox became merely a character in another logging era tall tale.

As I sat on the porch, I remembered meeting James Carter a couple of years ago and asking him about railways near Crooked Lake. He said that there might have been a temporary line in the area and asked me if I knew where the Haywire Trail, an ATV recreational trail, was. I said that I did (although I didn't tell him I drove along it to reach my secret blueberry patch). He said that it was built on the roadbed of the Manistique and Lake Superior Railroad. "It ended operations in 1968," he told me. "I happened to be driving by there on the evening it made its last run. I heard its whistle as it approached the highway. I stopped and watched the end of a piece of history."

Only a couple of faint whistle blasts carried on the cool air of this late spring night. But they brought back wonderful memories of my childhood and reminded me of some of the rich history of the area I now call home in the spring and summer.

A Little Night Music

On the nights when the north wind isn't blowing vigorously or music from a neighbor's place down the way doesn't pulsate loudly through the trees, there is no finer way to end a day at the lake than to fall asleep listening to the variegated sounds of nature's nocturnal symphony.

It usually begins around the time you're walking up from the lake after watching the setting of the sun. You hear a belch that seems as if it came from a creature much bigger than the tiny frog that produced it. An answer comes from the reeds a few feet away, and then another and another until there is a chorus that would make Aristophanes proud.

Occasionally, there'll be a special performance—the multi-note yipping of a group of coyotes. Are they happily welcoming a family member back to the group? Are they warning off bigger predators? How many of them are there? Individual coyotes have the ability to produce different vocalizations very rapidly, one after the other. When we think we're listening to an ensemble, we could actually be hearing a virtuoso solo.

When a front moves in, you are awakened by the distant rumble of thunder and the freshening of the breeze. A pine cone will drop on the roof and roll down to the ground and a spruce branch will rub against the shed. At first, we can hear individual drops of rain on the skylight and then what sounds like a waterfall.

In the quiet after the brief storm, we hear the most wonderful sound of the night, the aria of a loon calling to a mate who is back on the nest.

Of course, not all the night sounds are welcomed. The monotonous whine of a horde of mosquitoes clinging to the outside of the screen tempts us to close the window. It's as pleasant as listening to the strings warming up in the orchestra pit. And there is nothing more annoying than the buzz of a lone female around your ears just as you are about to drift off.

As the gray of dawn gradually dims the stars, the nocturnal symphony is replaced by an aubade. In the distance, the raucous squawks of some sandhill cranes announce that they are departing to their feeding ground along the edges of the highway. A gaggle of crows engage in a conference of grave importance. And, in front of the cabin, a robin chirps, before running a few steps and cocking its head to listen for worms.

A new day is beginning with its own wonderful natural music. It's time to get up and enjoy the world outside.

5 Flowers, Trees, and Stumps

The calendar on our kitchen wall, colorfully illustrated with pictures of Upper Peninsula scenic spots, denotes the solstice and equinox dates. But people at the lake know that, although the dates are fixed, the seasons don't always arrive as scheduled. The blooming of certain flowers and the changing colors of the leaves on the trees across the lake are far better indicators of the progress of the seasons. And, if we want to look into the historical and mythic past of our lake, we don't need books; we only have to gaze at the cedar stumps that line the shore and the lilies that float atop the water in the lake's swampy spots.

A Tuft of Flowers

I arrived at Crooked Lake last Thursday, the earliest I've come here in nearly a quarter of a century. Oh what a difference showing up three or four weeks earlier than usual makes.

As I drove down the dusty back road, I could see for what seemed like miles and miles through the trees. Virtually none of the leaves were out and there was no ground cover. The woods looked like a not-too-well manicured park.

After I'd unpacked and watered the dogs, I headed down to the lake to survey the scene I'd visited in my mind countless times during the last eight months. Across the lake, bare tree trunks, white for the birches and gray for the popples and maples, stood as a reminder of what the lake's shores must have looked like throughout the long winter.

But there were signs that spring had just arrived. A pale green sheen surrounded the birch branches and a rusty-bronze the maples. These

Fig. 5-1: Forget-Me-Nots

were the newly "hatched" (as we used to say when we were kids) leaves, just a day or so before the end of their bud stage.

On the near shore, white, delicate blossoms adorned the service-berry bushes—the first of the season's flowers. In fact, petals had already begun to drop, their white flakes resting beside the tiny star flowers that had pushed through the carpet of brown leaves and red pine needles.

Four very warm days have brought spring with a rush. The birch and maple leaves are turning a deeper green and you can hardly see the branches and trunks. Stalks of bracken fern, which had just begun to push their fiddle-head tops above the ground the day I arrived, have grown a foot or more into the spring air.

One of the first jobs after unpacking the car, tidying up the cabin, and putting in the boat is cleaning up around the outside of the cabin: raking last autumn's leaves (where the black flies like to live), clearing away branches blown down during winter storms, and cutting the grasses and weeds of spring.

One year, when Carol saw me coming out of the shed with the weed-whacker (manual) and rake, she took me to a spot just behind the cabin and pointed out a tuft of forget-me-nots, tiny powder blue flowers with yellow centers. "Cut around them if you can," she asked. "I really like them."

It was Carol's last summer at the lake. But every summer since then, I've been very careful when clearing around the forget-me-nots. This year, there were five clumps of the flowers. I made sure they were not harmed. While I carefully worked around them, I remembered that happy summer of many years ago.

The Flowers that Bloom in Late Spring, Tra La

The flowers that greeted me when I arrived at the lake three weeks ago are gone. The serviceberry petals have fallen like isolated snowflakes. The wild strawberry blossoms have disappeared, but left behind a promise of my usual harvest of six or eight of the sweet little berries.

The pussy toes, with their furry strands, have gone on little cat feet, and the purple gay wings have lost their luster and are about to fly away.

These are what Charlotte Cavattica would have called humble flowers because they grow close to the ground. Only the gay wings, looking like miniature orchids, called attention to themselves; the rest were very demure. They seemed shy as they bloomed just an inch or so above the ground still covered by last autumn's leaves. But they brought with them the promise of summer sunshine.

Then, last week, I saw the first of the taller flowers that would replace these harbingers of long, warm days. It was a lady slipper at the end of the neighbor's driveway. My flower book includes it in a chapter on pink and red flowers. But it seemed a dull gray-purple to me. It looked as bashful as its predecessors, wearing a color that seemed designed not to draw attention to itself. Its head bowed toward the ground, as if, like the tallest kid in the elementary classroom, it was embarrassed to be towering above the other flowers.

The forget-me-nots are flourishing like I've never seen before. And the dandelions—well, they were here when I first showed up in mid-May and they'll probably still be here when I leave after Labor Day.

This morning, I saw the most wonderful promise of summer: a solitary delicate, shy pink wild rose blooming on the bank by the water. Every morning, after I'd put the coffee on, I used go to the water's edge, pick a bud and put it in a small brandy snifter, which I placed on the kitchen table. Then Carol and I would sip our coffee and gaze at the glass to see if we could spot the petals opening.

The Names of Trees

When I was a little kid, I grouped trees into three categories. Christmas trees (all the evergreens that grew what we generically called pine cones), maples (we learned the words to the patriotic Canadian song "The Maple Leaf Our Emblem Dear" in first grade), and all the rest.

A few trees had special names. There was the Straight Arrow tree, an aging cedar that had a hollow near the base in which I hid my homemade bow and arrows. The Tarzan tree, an alder, had a large branch overhanging the trail. I used to crouch on it, rubber knife clenched in my teeth, ready to spring on the back of Numa the Lion (really our pet spaniel) as she stalked my sisters, sunbathing on the beach. Second Base was an enormous Douglas fir located in the middle of the large dirt parking lot that served as our baseball diamond for pickup games among the cousins. The back part of it (right behind the pitcher's mound) was second base.

When I worked for the British Columbia Forest Service during high school and college summers, I had to become much more specific. I learned to spot the differences between a Douglas fir, Balsam, and Hemlock and between a Monticola and a Ponderosa pine.

One of our crew was taking forestry at the university and taught us the Latin names of the trees that surrounded us. I thought this was great and, when I went back to university in the fall (as an English major), I thought I'd impress one of the girls in the dorm with my newly-acquired knowledge. As we walked through the woods on the way to the beach on a Saturday afternoon, I pointed out a Douglas fir. "That's *a pseudotsugamenziezi*."

"Oh," she replied.

I identified other trees and received equally bored responses. But then, I saw a magnificent Ponderosa pine. Surely, she'd be interested in the intricate jigsaw puzzle-like designs of the bark. "That's *a pinus ponderosa*. Come and look." Unfortunately, I'd mispronounced the first name of the species. She turned around and walked back to the dorm in a huff.

When we moved east and began spending time at Crooked Lake, I had the opportunity to learn the names of trees I hadn't been familiar with back in British Columbia. There was the American beech, the paper birch, and the magnificent eastern white pine. (I didn't bother to learn the Latin names.)

We gave some of the individual trees along the shoreline or the backwoods trails their own names. There was the rooster tree, a giant hemlock with a top like a perched rooster; the spitting tree, a white pine that seemed to be spitting on you when you sat under it; and the woodpecker tree, a lake-side cedar that each year had more and more almost rectangular holes bored into it.

Our favorite over the years has been the small hemlock that clings tenaciously to the bank at the edge of the lake. It's only about 20 feet tall—in fact, it doesn't seem to have grown much in the nearly four decades we've been coming here. But there it is in very late spring when we open up the cabin, an old friend we look forward to seeing each year.

In the late afternoon, when the sun shines just right on the water, the tree stands silhouetted, its top tipped over, its trunk leaning slightly to the north in its quest for sunlight. It reminds us of Canadian painter Tom Thomson's famous depiction of a Jack pine, a hardy survivor in Ontario's rugged north woods. Our tree really doesn't look that much like the pine in the painting, but it seems to have the same spirit.

We call it the Tom Thomson tree, and it's our favorite tree ever.

Requiem for a Cedar and Some Beeches

One peaceful June day, the angry snarl of a chainsaw and the heavy throbbing motor of a small earthmoving machine broke the silence.

Late in the afternoon, after the operator of the chainsaw and bobcat had left, I sauntered along the shore path to see what had been going on. In front of one of the cabins to the north of us, the bobcat's tread marks led to the water's edge. The railroad ties that the Forest Service had placed along the bank against erosion had been pulled away and a long, sloping ramp cut through the sand.

That evening, walking along the back road, I discovered what the chainsaw had been used for. Something had been dragged along the two-track and then into the woods away from the lake. I followed a trail of broken ferns and found a freshly cut Eastern White cedar. It wasn't very big, perhaps eight inches in diameter, but that didn't mean it was a young tree. Eastern whites are slow-growing, living for hundreds of years. This one was probably older than the cabin owner who'd had it cut down.

I was annoyed that the Forest Service regulations, designed to protect the fragile lake-side environment, had been blatantly ignored. And I was saddened that a tree that the Anishinaabe (Ojibway) people considered sacred had been destroyed. For them it was a gift, a bringer of building materials and medicines and they called it "nookomisgiizhik," Grandmother Cedar, a term of reverence and respect.

The cedar was also a gift to the animals and white settlers. Deer ate its "leaves" during winter; the newcomers to the land used the wood for log cabins, shingles, and support beams. But the fellers of this cedar didn't even save it to use as kindling to start the roaring campfires they sometimes held late into the nights. It was left to wither and die, unnoticed by anyone but me.

The Anishinaabe believed that all living things had souls. May the soul of 'nookomisgiizhik," grandmother cedar, find peace.

A few weeks later, I again heard the angry snarl of chainsaws. I'd been walking around Colwell Lake when I came across some Forest Service employees felling several beech, beautiful, tall, smooth-barked trees referred to in the Celtic tradition as "Queen Mothers of the Woods." They symbolized sustenance and preservation. Called "au zhaw way mish" by the Anishinaabe, their leaves were used for medicinal purposes and the nuts as food.

But these beech were dying of a disease that was spreading rapidly. "Some campers had brought some diseased firewood into the campsite and later abandoned it," one of the Forest Service people explained. "That's why there are all those signs about not transporting firewood from somewhere else. It gives deadly arboreal diseases a free ride." Beech makes great firewood. But this wouldn't be given to campers: "They might take it somewhere else and spread the disease. We have to burn all of this right here and now."

I left hoping that it wouldn't spread to the beech stands behind our cabins. But, the next summer, it had arrived, and once again I heard the angry snarl of chainsaws. Like "nookomisgiizhik", "au zhaw way mish" has perished, a victim of human beings. We are all poorer for their deaths and the thoughtlessness that caused them.

Stumps

I have become fascinated with stumps. It all began three winters ago when I was doing research on later 19th century logging in Michigan's Upper Peninsula. I came across an article about the Kingston Plains, which are located about 25 miles northeast of my cabin. The area was one of the sites of clear cutting as an army of axe wielders advanced westward across northern Michigan in the 1880s.

The article had photographs of the area the way it looks now. In acres and acres of fields huge stumps stand in silent testimony to the great pine forests that are no more.

The next summer, my friend Deb LeBlanc, who knows as much about the flora and fauna of the UP as anyone I've met, took me to the Kingston Plains. It was an amazing sight: so many stumps, all of them enormous. Some were six feet high, an indication of how deep the snows had been during the winter during which they'd been felled. The centers are decayed, but most were remarkably well preserved. Some had survived fires, as indicated by the black marks on them. "Awesome" is an overused word. But walking through the fields was an awesome experience. Since then, a trip to the Kingston Plains has been a regular stop on sightseeing trips with our visitors. All have been amazed by what one of them called "the graveyard of trees."

Fig. 5-2: "The Graveyard of Trees"

My visits to the Kingston Plains have made me become much more sensitive to the stumps around our cabin. As I walked the path along the shore, I began to notice the cedar stumps almost hidden by the summer bracken. When the trees were cut, they were probably floated to the north end of Crooked Lake, loaded on a logging train and taken over a temporary railroad line to the mill at Shingleton. Some of the cedar shakes that covered the roofs of houses in cities far away probably came from the trees along Crooked Lake's shores.

This spring, before the bracken rose up, I made a wonderful discovery as I was walking out behind the cabin. I noticed, for the first time, an enormous stump. Even in its decayed condition, it was probably four feet in diameter.

It was all that remained of a great white pine which had no doubt been felled in the 1880s. Even judging from the diminished size of the stump, it must have been at least 250 years old when its life ended. That would have meant it was a seedling in the early 1600s, a time long before successive waves of Europeans swept over the UP. I wondered what it would have been like before the UP was surveyed and the loggers and miners arrived to have walked among the giants of the Kingston Plains or even those near the shores of Crooked Lake.

Of course, an experience like that will never be possible. But as I view the stumps of the Kingston Plains and even "my stump," I can sense the ghosts of a magnificent landscape that once was.

Star Maidens on the Lake

Last night, we stayed up unusually late, sitting around the campfire sharing memories, many of them enhanced by the passage of time and a few sips of wine. When everyone started yawning, we doused the fire and took a final walk down to the dock.

It was a clear and moonless night. As we gazed upward, we were awed, as we always are, by the sheer number of stars and began engaging in those existential questions that seem to arise at such moments. How far away are the most distant of stars we can see? Have some of the ones that twinkle tonight died thousands upon thousands of years ago? Is some intelligent being way out there looking at Earth and wondering if there is intelligent life here?

The recognizable constellations stood out against what almost seemed like a thin muslin background. A couple of the more experienced sky gazers identified star groups the others had only heard of and still couldn't clearly perceive. Of course, everyone recognized the Big Dipper, but we were surprised when another member of the party said that it was made up of eight stars, not just the seven visible to the naked eye. We all looked through the binoculars and noticed a very tiny one next to one of the bigger ones on the handle. "There's a Lakota [Sioux] legend," he told us, "about seven brothers and their little sister who fled to the sky to escape a dangerous situation and became what we call the Big Dipper."

A few moments later, someone spotted a shooting star that seemed to disappear behind the point where Native artifacts have been discovered by archaeologists. That put me in mind of a wonderful Anishinaabe (Ojibway) story I'd heard many years ago. I didn't repeat it to the group because it was sacred property of the Native peoples and like most sacred narratives should not be told in the summer. But quite simply, it was about a star maiden who wanted to live near human beings and, after rejecting several locations, chose a lake near people whose lifestyles and cultural values she greatly admired. She became a white water lily and, finding peace and joy, invited her sisters to join her as lake blossoms.

As I drifted off to sleep, I thought about the legend and the shooting star and remembered that on the other side of the point there was a large field of water lilies. Everyone else slept in late the next morning, But an hour after daybreak, I slipped out of the house, launched the canoe, and paddled in the stillness to the spot where the lilies bloomed. As I coasted toward the myriad star-shaped white flowers, I allowed myself to believe that last night's shooting star had landed here, bringing another celestial maiden who wanted to share her life with the many creatures of the earth and to live in peace and harmony with them.

I heard the lap of tiny ripples against the canoe, the croak of a distant frog, and the whine of a mosquito. Along the shore behind the lilies, a heron stood motionless. I felt a wonderful sense of harmony with the lake and its creatures. I understood why the star maiden had chosen a spot like this to live on earth. And I hoped that shooting stars would continue to bring her descendants to Crooked Lake and other lakes in the Upper Peninsula. I paddled back around the point and east toward the sun which had risen above the tree line.

Pines and Birches

Many years ago, I noticed an unusual natural formation at the end of one of the driveways at the lake. Sprouting from the rotting stump of a long-dead white pine were three birch saplings. The pine had likely been felled in the 1890s, harvested as part of the logging boom of that era. The birches, likely four or five years old, were drawing nourishment from the remains of the forest giant. The stump, much diminished, is still there, and the saplings now reach over 40 feet into the air, healthy and mature trees in the prime of their life cycles.

When I'd first noticed the pine and birches, I'd been studying the traditional legends of the Anishinaabe people and the tall tales about the logger Paul Bunyan. I thought the stump and saplings were emblems of two different cultures and their values. I still do.

The pine, the Latin name of which is *pinus strobes,* was one of countless thousands of the species felled across the upper Midwest in the later 19th century to provide lumber for dwellings and other buildings for the rapidly increasing numbers of European pioneers. As soon as an area was clear cut, the loggers moved on. There was at that time no plan for reforestation. The companies they worked for thought the sylvan bounty would never be exhausted. Now, however, there are a few stands of first-growth white pines still around, but they are carefully protected.

The paper birch, "wilgwaasaatig" to the Anishinaabe, was much faster-growing and shorter lived. The people used the bark, highly water repellant, as the outer covering for their canoes and dwellings. They took only what they needed. The birch was one of the trees for which they had great respect: it was a living fellow being with which they shared the land.

Around our lake, there are a few large white pines. They survived because they were forked and so considered dangerous to fell and of limited commercial value. The birch, in the meantime, was of little use to the lumber companies. But, as birches do, they quickly colonized the clear-cut areas. Nature was making a comeback.

To me, the stump and the three saplings are reminders of the legendary figures whose deeds and actions reflected the values of the people who told their stories. Paul Bunyan was a company man; his great strength and amazing feats were performed in the service of "progress," in which more and bigger and better were what civilization "needed." Nanabozho was a hero for a people who lived as a part of, not apart from, the natural world. He could do foolish things that violated the cultural norms. The lateral dark markings on the white birch bark are a reminder of one of his selfish actions. But the brilliant yellow of the tree's autumn leaves is a symbol of one of his greatest actions, the dangerous quest to bring fire to his people.

While the pine stumps slowly decay, the birches continue to regenerate from decade to decade. They are emblems of a way of life that saw nature as a community and not a commodity.

O Tannenbaum

When Christmas time arrives and we go to the local charity lot to pick our tree, my mind travels in space and time. In space to the Little Cabin in the Big Woods, now probably half buried in snow, but in my imagination illuminated by strings of lights we've put on the pine saplings that have grown up close to the walls. In time, back to my youth, when we made the final trip of the year up to the lake to harvest our tree. As my father described it in one of his columns, it was quite an expedition. Here's what he wrote:

For years, when our elder daughter was a little girl and her sister and brother were babies, selecting, cutting and bringing out the tree from Shawnigan was a major occasion. A week before Christmas, we'd drive up to the lake, pack down through woods dripping from rain or sparkling with frost to the one-roomed cabin.

Our first chore was to set the rusty old stove roaring with the dry wood kept under the house. Once assured of warmth indoors, small daughter and I would take the trail leading up to the railway tracks. She'd be snug in a hooded, royal blue snowsuit and yellow gumboots. I'd wear an old raincoat and old pants tucked into heavy socks above rubber boots.

She'd pick the tree. We'd circle it to check for balanced spacing of branches and usually reject the first selection because it almost always was bare on one side. Along the trail she'd shorten the way with bright chatter, telling me stories that came into her head as we trudged, and breaking off to shout, "There's one!" So we'd inspect the small fir she pointed to and, eventually, decide one was worth cutting. Since we provided trees for two or three friends in town, we had a few options. When the cut tree looked less attractive than it did growing, we'd look for something better for our living room.

When the twins grew older, we'd be a party of four and the difficulty of picking the tree was doubled. So was the problem of pulling small, warmly clad children from the underbrush where they'd strayed to pick an Oregon grape leaf that frost had turned scarlet. We gathered treasures along the way, made up our little stories, and sang "Heigh-ho, heigh-ho."

By the time our harvest was complete, we'd all be wet and grow wetter on the way down the hillside with our greenery. Invariably, as we crossed the small streamlet tinkling between us and the road, a small child would learn that the water ran to a depth over the top of a gumboot and that it was very cold. Small noses would grow cherry red, and hands, too, in their soaked woolen mittens.

Back at the cabin, we'd cluster around the stove. The youngsters would be stripped and snowsuits hung to warm, if not dry. Gumboots would be paired and propped upside down to absorb the heat, and mittens would be laid on the oven door. After hot soup and hot beans, we'd lash the trees to the car top and head home. A simple joy, the annual trip to the woods, merry with laughter in spite of the huge responsibility of picking the right tree.

Victoria Daily Times, December 24, 1970

6   Day Tripper

In the mornings, we often see chipmunks race across the path from one old tree stump to another. Experts say that these little animals have small ranges, half an acre at best. That means that the ones we see never go to visit the ones who live next door. Much of the time, we're like the chipmunks. When we're at the lake we stay pretty close to home, although we do visit with the neighbors. But a few times each summer, we wander much further afield, especially when we have guests. We like them to see some of our favorite UP places, most no more than an hour and a half drive from home base. We often conclude our excursions by visiting one of the local brewpubs for a lunch or a late afternoon snack, enjoying along with it beer that is brewed only a dozen or so yards from our table.

Seney National Wildlife Refuge: Returned to Nature

It's just four corners at the intersection of highways M-77 and M-28; but during the late 19th century, Seney was an incredibly important spring destination. The long, cold, dark winter over, legions of loggers would emerge from the bush, anxious to spend their winter's wages at the town's twenty-one saloons, five blind-pigs (illegal bars), and two brothels. It was one of the Upper Peninsula's notorious "hell towns in the pines."

Twelve decades later, the towering white pines, the loggers, and the brothels are all long gone. However, the area is still an important spring destination. Just under five miles south of Seney on M-77 is the entrance to the Seney National Wildlife Refuge, a 95,000 acre preserve, where thousands of migrating birds either spend a night or two resting before they continue to their summer homes further north or settle down here, nesting, mating, and then raising their young.

This landscape of ponds and bogs, rivers and ditches, grasslands and forests has gone through many transformations. After the logging era, the Western Land Surety Company, intending to sell agricultural plots, drained and cleared the land. But the soil, much of it peat and most of it sandy, was unsuitable for farming, and the State of Michigan reclaimed the area for back taxes. In 1935, the US Fish and Wildlife Service acquired the land and began a project of building dikes and controlling channels and ponds to create a habitat suitable for waterfowl. Since then, the area has been in a constant state of evolution. "We don't focus on creating an environment as much as restoring a natural environment," one of the park rangers explained to me a few years ago.

At one time, we used to drive our cars along dirt roads atop the many dykes. Now we usually stroll leisurely on the 1.7-mile Pine Ridge Nature Trail, a very informative and partly wheelchair accessible path around Upper F Pool near the visitor center.

Shortly after entering the trail, we notice a couple of trumpeter swans in a smaller pool to the right, floating majestically as they keep an eye on their nearby nest. A few steps further, a sign draws attention to a "Monarch Way Station." In the late summer, stalks of milkweed and other flowers attract the magnificent butterflies, offering sustenance on their long southern journey.

We take the time to read all the interpretive signs along the trail. They not only tell us what we're looking at, but also explain the interrelationship among the living beings that inhabit the spot. For example, the larch or tamarack (a deciduous tree that looks like an evergreen) can have its needles eaten by the larch sawfly, and sawfly larvae attract grosbeaks who find them quite a delicacy.

The wheelchair-accessible section of the trail ends at a large observation deck that gives views of the pond and beyond it a fire-spotting tower. At different times of the season, common loons (which were once a threatened species) raise their young here. There are mating pairs of loons on seventeen of the refuge's larger ponds. One of the males is a celebrity. ABJ (the initials stand for Adult Banded as a Juvenile) was born in 1987 and is the oldest loon of known age in the world.

The fire tower is a reminder that, even in the Refuge, much of which is wetland, fire is an ever-present danger. During the hot, dry summer of 1976, a lightning strike started what became one of the largest forest fires in Michigan history, covering over 78,000 acres. Although the damage to the land was great, the habitat has regenerated almost completely since then, an example of how one of the great forces of nature is an important part of a complicated eco-system.

The remainder of the loop is a narrow, winding dirt trail which passes marshy and thicketed areas that provide nesting areas for waterfowl, clumps of wild blueberry bushes enjoyed by bears, birds, and human passersby, and birch trees in which sap suckers have drilled holes to find the syrup that feeds them and hummingbirds. Occasionally, usually later in the day, strollers who lift their eyes to the sky may see one of the many bald eagles who call the Refuge their home returning from its daytime haunts, one of which is our lake over 20 miles, as the eagle flies, away.

The pathway leads back to the visitor center and parking lot. We leave, glad that we took the advice of one park ranger: "The Refuge is a subtle place—slow down and appreciate it."

DIRECTIONS: From the intersection of M-28 and M-77, head south 5 miles on M-77; the road to the Visitor Center is on the right.

Grand Marais: Life in a Pickle Barrel

Grand Marais, a small village and harbor nestled along the southern shore of Lake Superior, is one of my favorite places to take visitors. The trip from the cabin to the village passes through some picturesque and historic countryside and the destination is the home of Dunes Saloon and Lake Superior Brewing Company, one of the favorite watering holes of the well-known novelist, the late James Harrison. I've read a lot about this history of the place and about the writers who've lived there and, if I'm sure the visitors know very little about all this, I enjoy acting as the "knowledgeable" tour guide.

The "tour" begins as we drive east along highway M-28 from Shingleton to Seney. "This," I intone in my best tour-guide voice, "has been called the most boring road in America. Twenty-six miles without a curve. They had a marathon here, but only for a year. Three runners died ...[long pause] ... of boredom."

Turning north on highway M-77, we pass through country that was one of the centers of the long-ago logging boom. "Nearly all the logs ended up in Grand Marais, where, some people say, there were nearly a dozen mills operating near the end of the 19th century. Over two thousand people lived here then. Now it's just under 300 year around."

We cross over a bridge under which flows the Sucker River. "But where's the Two-Hearted River?" one of my guests, a former English major, asks. It was made famous by a 1920s short story by Ernest Hemingway. I explain that it's several miles to the east, but that the Sucker River was the real setting for the story. "Hemingway just changed the name to make it sound more symbolic." "But," I go on, "Jim Harrison had his summer home on the Sucker River."

When we arrive at the crest of the hill that overlooks the village of Grand Marais, everyone agrees that it's just like a New England seaside village. "I can't wait to walk around," another guest enthuses. "I read that there are four museums, and I love museums."

At the bottom of the hill, someone calls out: "Look over there. It looks like a giant wooden barrel." I agree and explain that it's one of the town's four museums.

"It's lunchtime," another tourist proclaims. "Let's go to the Dunes and then the Pickle Barrel. That's all I want to see." We agree. At lunch, as we enjoy a white fish sandwich and the blueberry wheat beer brewed on site, I point out the man working behind the bar. "He's Dave, the manager and brewer, and he has a bit role to play in some of Harrison's novels."

While we're eating, I give a short lecture on the history of the Pickle Barrel House. It was originally the summer home of William Donahey, a cartoonist who created a comic strip about the "Teenie Weenies," a group of little people who made use of normal-sized objects in their everyday life. One of their homes was a wooden pickle barrel, and Donahey had a human size replica of it built and shipped to his Upper Peninsula lake property for use as a summer cabin. After several years, he grew tired of the curious tourists who would knock on his door and ask for a tour and so he donated it to the town of Grand Marais. After service as a tourist shop, ice cream store, and gift shop, it stood empty before the Grand Marais Historical Society took it over and turned it into a museum.

Our tour didn't take that long. Inside the front door, there is a small souvenir/gift stand. Period furniture is placed around the rest of the first floor and vintage portraits of the Donaheys adorn the curving walls. On one side, a narrow staircase leads to the second floor where there are two small beds, a dresser, and bedside tables. A pantry connects the larger, 20-foot-high barrel to a slightly smaller one, which housed a kitchen, with a small stove, small table, and two chairs.

As we leave, one of our guests asks: "What did they do when they had guests who stayed over?"

"They probably found themselves in a real pickle," the tour guide says, smiling at his self-perceived cleverness.

DIRECTIONS: From the intersection of M-24 and M-77 travel north 25 miles on M-77 to Grand Marais. The Pickle Barrel Museum is at the bottom of the hill at the south end of town.

Au Sable Point: To the Lighthouse

This afternoon, I stopped at Hurricane River Campground to take my favorite Lake Superior shore stroll: the 1.7 mile dirt road that runs beside the beach and stretches from the campground east to the Au Sable Light Station.

It was a perfect late summer day, sunny, temperature in the low 70s, a gentle breeze blowing. The trail was through an area forested with many of the trees found throughout the UP: spruce, cedar, balsam and hemlock; aspen, maple, and birch. Through them, the ripples on the big lake sparkled in the sun. Here and there large trees had fallen from the bank across the sandy beach.

The road wasn't crowded: couples, families pushing strollers, a man walking with his dog. They were amblers—in no hurry, as they enjoyed the weather and the scenery. Five minutes along the way, a group of serious hikers with heavy backpacks strode determinedly toward the west. We chatted as they paused and leaned upon their sturdy walking poles. They'd left Grand Marais this morning on the beginning of a three-day hike to Munising. The 1.7 mile trail from the campground to the lighthouse is part of the North Country Trail, which begins in Vermont and meanders through eight states before ending in North Dakota.

The only really strenuous activity occurred a hundred or so yards ahead of me. A young woman in shorts and a sleeveless blouse was waving her arms wildly about her. She wasn't practicing semaphore, but trying to drive away a cloud of Stable Flies, late season successors to black, horse, and deer flies who are not driven off by insect repellant. Fortunately, I'd been forewarned and had on long pants and a long-sleeved shirt, heavy stocks under my boots, and a beekeeper's hat with a mesh screen to pull over my face and neck.

I passed a family that included two children who had been energetically running about for the first ten minutes after leaving the campground, but had slowed down. "Are we there yet?" came a plaintive voice. "I'm tired." It turned out that we were nearly there. At the end of a stretch of the road with a canopy of green leaves arching over it loomed the white tower of the Au Sable Light Station standing out against the cloudless blue sky background.

Built in 1873, it's one of nine lighthouses between Whitefish Point to the east and Grand Island (near Munising) to the west and is still operational (although now automated). As I often do when I visit, I paid the three dollars to make the escorted tour up the hundred steps to the top. I need the exercise, and on a clear day like today, the view is amazing. One of the windows looks to the east and the Grand Sable Dunes, a sandy slope that descends 300 feet to the lakeshore. There used to be a lookout platform there, but it collapsed a couple of winters ago, the victim of high, fierce winter winds that eroded the foundation on which it was built. The north window of the tower gives a view over the lake. Today, the reef of sandstone, which in some places is only six feet under water and extends a mile out from shore, is clearly visible. The light, which on clear nights is visible 16 miles away, warns boats away from the dangerous shoals.

But not all. The shore had been nicknamed the "Graveyard Coast." A National Parks Service brochure lists twenty-two "viewable" wrecks between Grand Marais and Grand Island. I saw three of them when I decided to return to the parking lot along the beach itself. Today, the people on the beach were enjoying Lake Superior at its summer best. A few dozen yards away were examples of the destructive power of the lake that many of the locals call "Mother Superior." Near them were the ribs and heavy spikes of wrecked ships, half buried in the sand like the bones of some long-ago beached leviathan. The *Mary Jarecki* had lost its course during a fog and ran aground in 1883; the *Sitka*, a victim of high winds and fog, ran aground in 1904; and the *Gale Staples* was driven off course by high winds in1918.

Walking along the shoreline was fun, but when stretches of wet and slippery sandstone replaced the sand, I decided it was time to go back to the trail and head to the parking lot. As I passed through the campground I waved to the hiking group as they set up their tents.

Fig. 6-1: Au Sable Light Station

Maybe I'll see them when I go to town in a couple of days.

DIRECTIONS: From Grand Marais, take highway H-58 west to the Hurricane River Campground. The dirt road to the Au Sable Light Station begins at the eastern edge of the campground.

Sand Point Marsh Trail: Munising's Beautiful Swamp

Swamps have undeservedly acquired bad reputations. Maybe it's because of those 1950s horror movies where creatures emerged from the ooze, glop streaming down their scaly bodies as they crept stealthily toward helpless young white women. Or maybe it's because politicians describe the political landscape as an unhealthy morass created by members of the other party, but which they will take the responsibility of draining. However, they are mistaking swamps for cesspools. The former are natural parts of a healthy landscape; the latter are toxic pits filled with manmade filth and slime. Drain the cesspools, but save the swamps.

I thought about these things this morning while I made the first of the frequent walks I take each year along the (completely wheelchair accessible) Sand Point Marsh Trail. It's a half-mile boardwalk trail above a wetlands four miles northwest of Munising. It's important that the trail is built above the marsh: people can view and contemplate without invading and interfering with the delicate ecosystem. It was built in the summer of 1989 by the Youth Conservation Corps and the staff of the Pictured Rocks National Lakeshore and provides people with a chance to observe not nature restored or recreated, but nature as it has been for centuries.

You park facing the East Channel, the stretch of Lake Superior that runs between the mainland and Grand Island. On a hot summer day, the beach in front of you will be teeming with young children playing in the sand and splashing in the never-warm water. Across the water, you'll see the East Channel Lighthouse, built in 1868 and decommissioned just before World War I. A wooden structure, the walls and tower weathered gray by decades of exposure to wind, rain, and snow, it seems like a venerable old church watching over the boats that pass by it.

Crossing the road away from the lake, you watch out for the dozens of cars that pass daily, many of them on their way to Sand Point where there is a maritime museum, another sandy beach, and the first view of the Pictured Rocks National Lakeshore. Then you take a short path that leads you to the marsh trail, the existence of which is probably unknown to most of the tourists headed to the point. Although you can hear the occasional shrieks of the youthful swimmers and the sounds of the passing vehicles, it's as if you have entered a separate and separated world. In a sense you have—the world of a swamp, an interrelated, natural community.

There are plenty of interpretive signs along with observation decks and benches along the way—places to stand or sit and stare, listen, and smell and to contemplate the apparently simple, but truly complex world you've entered. The first "rest-stop" offers a view across one of the ponds to the cliffs to the east, cliffs that are the end (or beginning) of bluffs that become the Pictured Rocks. If you're quiet and still, especially in the morning early in the season, you may see a blue heron, a mink, or a garter snake. Any time of day you can see the large, tangled root systems of pine, cedar, spruce, or hemlock trees that have blown over in high winds and been left on the ground and in the water to return to nature. At the edge of one of the ponds are charred stumps, survivors of fires that are part of the natural processes of life and death in the swamp.

One of the interpretive signs commemorates the Anishinaabe (known to many as the Chippewa or Ojibway), who have lived in the area for over 300 years. It explains how the wetland plants and animals provided materials for building and for making clothing, along with food and medicine. Depending on the season, there will be white water lilies, blue iris, and pale pink wild roses (the dried hips of which were collected in the fall and used to make Native tea). On a summer day, frogs swim through the shallows, while turtles sun themselves on half-submerged logs. When the trail leaves the marsh, it passes through many blueberry bushes and you can stop and gather a handful of the tiny fruits for a snack.

At the end of the trail, just where the North Country Trail heads off to the east, there is a sobering sign. "Nearly half of the eastern Upper Peninsula of Michigan is wetland. Although this seems like a lot of land, Michigan has already lost 71 per cent of its original wetlands." The sign then remarks how important places like the Sand Point Marsh are to healthy eco-systems. "Only people can preserve wetlands. People like you."

In other words, don't drain the swamp. Cherish it and protect it—for the sake of the well-being of all the interrelated communities it nourishes.

DIRECTIONS: From the traffic circle at the edge of Munising, head four miles east along East Munising Avenue and then north along Sand Point Road to the parking lot beside the swimming beach. The marsh trail is across the road.

Marquette's Lakenenland: Not Just Another Roadside Attraction

In our family, we're not big fans of roadside attractions, especially the ones with very large signs proclaiming they are "World Famous." Our aversion explains why, for over 15 years after it opened in 2003, we always drove past "Lakenenland" on our way to or from Marquette.

Then, one day, our neighbors, who had stopped and toured place, enthusiastically told us about it. "It's hard to describe—you really have to see it for yourself." They did, however, tell us about the roadside attraction's back story. Tom Lakenen, an iron worker, had made the decision to stop spending his evenings, weekends, and winter layoff periods sitting on a bar stool and to find a creative hobby. He started scrounging pieces of discarded metal and rusty old equipment and transforming them into "Junkyard Art:" metal sculptures that often evoke smiles and chuckles and frequently convey important social messages.

When his garage/workshop and backyard began to overflow with his creations, he purchased land 13 miles east of Marquette that lay between highway M-28 and the North Country Trail, bulldozed a winding road through the pines and began placing his statues, which range from three to nearly 20 feet high, among the trees. Each year he added new ones and, as of 2021, there were over one hundred of them.

Since we made our first stop a few years ago, a visit to Lakenenland has become a regular part of our trips to Marquette. You can drive through the half-mile art trail, but we prefer to saunter, pausing to stand and stare at leisure at old favorites and recent additions. And, if our legs get a little tired, there are benches along the trail where we can sit and, like patrons at a gallery, gaze at length at the art before us.

Our favorites are whimsical pieces, tributes to heroes local and national, statues that make social commentary, and others that recall earlier eras of the UP. Near the start of the trail there's a Halloween statue with a witch on a broom, a ghost about to float away, and bats swooping around. Shortly after, we pass the bandstand where the "Rusty Chain Saw Band" is performing. Guess what the strings of their instruments are made of.

One of my favorite statues is a very large, rusty, cast-iron tank transformed into a pink pig identified as a "Genuine North American Greed Pig." It's pooping on a tiny person labeled "the American worker."

The parts of my leisurely stroll that I most enjoy are through what I've dubbed "The Avenue of Heroes" and "The Lane of History." There are tributes to the Marines, local firefighters and nurses, and—a recent addition—to the governor of Michigan, who faced death threats when she imposed strict regulations to protect people from the ravages of the COVID epidemic.

The first piece of "Junkyard Art" on "The Lane of History" is a portrait of a Native American, with the caption "Imagine When." Then there is a sign asking: "Take Take Take—How Long Will It Last?" Alongside the road are a caged animal, pieces of abandoned mining equipment, an empty farm wagon, and two loggers with a cross-cut saw—all emblems of vanished or disappearing elements of Upper Peninsula life.

Each time I visit Lakenenland, I think of the old saying, "One man's junk is another man's treasure." Tom Lakenen has salvaged junk metal and transformed it into a treasure that he generously (admission is free, but donations are gratefully accepted) shares with those who take the time visit what is definitely not just another roadside attraction.

DIRECTIONS: Take highway M-28for 13 miles east from Marquette. Lakenenland is on the south side of the highway. Look for the yellow crane.

Fayette: The UP's "Museum Village"

Today, we visited a tiny peninsula located on a bigger peninsula that juts southward from the Big Peninsula—the UP. It wasn't just a sightseeing outing along the southern shores of the Upper Peninsula, down the Garden Peninsula, and onto a small piece of land protruding westward into Lake Michigan. It was a journey into the past.

Our destination was Fayette Historic Park, what has been called a "museum village," a restoration of what, in the later 19th century, had been one of the Upper Peninsula's busiest and most important industrial centers. The Jackson Iron Company, seeking a way to reduce the costs of transporting the raw ore from its Negaunee mine to the great industrial cities of the lower Midwest, decided to send the ore by rail across the UP to Escanaba and then by barge to the town of Fayette, where it would be transformed into pig iron and then shipped south.

Fayette was an ideal location: it had relatively temperate weather all year around, a deep and safe harbor, limestone cliffs from which could be made mortar used in building the brick blast furnaces, and a nearby supply of maple and beech that could be transformed into charcoal to heat the furnaces. The first pig iron was produced on Christmas Day 1867 and the last shipped on December 1, 1891. By that time, the supplies of hardwood had been drastically reduced, the cost of refined iron had dropped considerably, and newer, more efficient smelting processes had been developed in many industrial cities of the Midwest. Thereafter, Fayette had been sporadically used as a summer resort area until the 1950s, when it was purchased by the State of Michigan, which began the long process of painstakingly restoring the surviving buildings. The restoration is still in process today.

We began our stroll in what is known as Fayette's Industrial Area, which includes the limestone kilns, the brick walls of the enormous blast furnaces, and the docks where raw iron was unloaded and pig iron loaded. The pilings from the 19th century docks remain; however, new docks at which tourists berth their pleasure crafts have replaced them. As I was looking out over the harbor at the white limestone cliffs towering above the shore to the north, one of these boats backed up from the wharf and began making large circles, bouncing off its own waves. Loud 1980s music blared from its cabin. I wondered if its skipper bothered to look at the giant brick buildings where some of the materials that contributed to the country's progress had been smelted.

The "museum village" is just that. Over a half century, the restoration of the buildings has been based on meticulous research. There are service buildings such as blacksmith shops, along with office buildings, a hotel (with a second story outhouse), a school house, an opera house, a general store, and, not much of a surprise, a jail. The various buildings are furnished with period pieces and equipment.

My favorite part of the excursion was a 20-minute stroll from the commercial, administrative center up the hill to a road circling the tip of the peninsula and then around to the southern beach. What I saw along the way explained the dynamics of what was completely a company town. On the hillside, set among trees, sheltered from the north winds and usually upwind from the smelters, were the homes of the superintendent, doctor, and higher level "white" collar administrators. Several white frame-houses had verandas that looked over gardens, across the harbor, to the blast furnaces.

On the southern side of the town were the crudely built log cabins in which lived the over 200 laborers and their families. The dwellings were simple and they were downwind from the smelters. They did have south-facing lake views and a beach. But it wasn't a sandy beach. The shoreline was covered with "slag," the waste byproduct of the smelting process. Even if the tenants of the log cabins had wanted to let their children swim or fetch buckets of water to use in the unplumbed dwellings, it wouldn't have been safe to do so. The water would have been seriously polluted by the "slag." Not only did these people live downwind from the smelter, their houses bore the full brunt of winter gales from the south.

The era of the iron ore industry that Fayette Historic Park celebrates is long gone, as are the owners and shareholders of the Jackson Iron Company, who lived far from the UP mines and smelters, as are the laborers who performed backbreaking labor so that the owners and shareholders could receive annual dividends.

As I drove back home across the Garden Peninsula, I thought of something that was there before Fayette was built and has survived longer than the kilns and smelters, the commercial and administrative buildings, the frame houses and log cabins. At the beginning of my stroll, I'd read a sign drawing attention to the cedar trees growing out of the limestone cliffs, clinging tenaciously to the soil. One of them was reported to be over 1400 years old. The iron ore era had come and gone, but was celebrated by the developers of the historic park. The cedars of Fayette have survived, noticed by few, but a testimony of the enduring powers of nature.

DIRECTIONS: From the Garden Corners intersection of highway US-2 and Highway M-183 (16 miles west of Manistique), head 17 miles south on M-183 to Fayette Historic State Park.

The Ale at the End of the Trail

Between 1973 and 1994, no beer was brewed commercially in the Upper Peninsula. Then, in the latter year, Michigan state laws made it possible to open brewpubs in which patrons could enjoy both beer and food created on the premises. Six of these opened by the end of the 20th century, including three close to the destinations of our day trips: Hereford and Hops of Escanaba (1994), Lake Superior Brewing Company of Grand Marais (1994), and Vierling Restaurant and Marquette Harbor Brewery (1995). By the beginning of the third decade of this century, the total number of craft breweries and brew-pubs in the Upper Peninsula had grown to twenty-eight, ten of them within a ninety-minute drive of our cabin.

There are many reasons we like including craft breweries and brewpubs in our day trips and shopping expeditions. First, they usually have local owners. Second, they offer an interesting variety of beers, not just the pale American lagers that have dominated the American scene over the past half century. On one visit to a brewpub, a member of our party remarked: "These taste different." To which came the reply: "Yes, they *have* taste!" There is a wide variety of pale ales, India Pale Ales, wheat beers, stouts, porters, amber ales, and the new favorites, sour beers, to name just a few. They often use local ingredients. The water, of course—which more than one brewer has told me, both jokingly and seriously, is truly superior—is local. Some of the brewers use locally grown hops, malt made from local grains, and even wild yeasts harvested from nearby forests and beaches.

These places aren't dark, dingy, roadhouses. Lake Superior Brewing in Grand Marais has tables with displays of local agates. You can see Lake Superior from the windows. The Vierling in Marquette was the home of a late 19th century bar and is decorated in period pieces. Window tables look out onto the Marquette Inner Harbor, which is dominated by a towering (and decommissioned) ore dock. In Escanaba, Hereford and Hops, established by a local breeder of beef cattle, is in a building on the National Register of Historic Sites. Begun as a luxury hotel, it was also a home for the elderly. Restored to its original glory, it houses a brewpub, a fine dining area, and other eating options. You can't see the water from the place, but you can build up an appetite or walk off a good meal by strolling a few blocks down Ludington Street to Lake Michigan to the lighthouse and museum.

Not all the brewery tap rooms we like to visit offer food, although they allow you to bring your own, send out, or, occasionally, order from food trucks parked nearby. That's the case with Ore Dock, Barrel and Beam, and Blackrocks in Marquette, and Upper Hand in Escanaba.

Visiting one of these craft breweries makes a great finish to a day trip. Of course, we have to drive home and so, if we want to sample a variety of beers, we order a flight, a tray of four or five very small glasses, each with a different style of beer. One time, we were at the Vierling when the man at the table next to us ordered a flight of ten. When it arrived, he gazed at it like a kid looking through the window of a candy store. He took a couple of sips from each glass, but didn't finish any of them. Then, he jokingly asked if he could take the leftovers home in a doggy bag, but the humorless server said that the law wouldn't allow it.

Frequently we take some beer home from the places we visit. All fill growlers (64 ounce glass bottles); some have crowlers (32 ounce cans filled from one of the taps and then capped and sealed). Ore Dock, Blackrocks, and Upper Hand package many of their beers in six packs. The growlers and crowlers don't stay fresh too long (a couple of days at best). But that's fine. If the weather's good the day after one of our excursions, we sit on the dock, sip a glass of beer, nosh on our leftover food and reminisce about our recent excursion.

Here's a list of brewpubs and brewery tap rooms that we enjoy visiting in Alger, Delta, Schoolcraft and Marquette Counties.

- **Marquette County**: Lake Superior Smokehouse and Brewpub (Chocolay Township), Drifa Brewing, Vierling Restaurant and Marquette Harbor Brewery, Ore Dock Brewery, Blackrocks Brewery, Barrel + Beam Brewery (all Marquette)

- **Delta County**: Hereford and Hops Steak House and Brewpub, Upper Hand Brewery (both Escanaba)

- **Schoolcraft County**: LaTulip Brewery (Cooks)

- **Alger County**: Lake Superior Brewing Company at Dunes Saloon (Grand Marais), By George Brewery, East Channel Brewery (both Munising).

7   On the Dock of the Bay

Fig. 7-1: This dock was made for sitting

The cabin is cozy, the blueberry picking is satisfying, and the day trips are entertaining. But the lake is the center of our summers. It's why we drive days to reach it each year. When we arrive, we rush down the path to see that it is still there. The last thing we do before getting into the car to begin the long drive back to the city of the pavements gray is to stand on the dock and say goodbye to it. In the weeks in between, we spend much time on it, in it, and sitting on the dock gazing at it.

Paddle to the Past

This morning, I took a short paddle in the canoe. I was only gone for 20 minutes, but I'd travelled four centuries into the past.

There was hardly any wind, no one else was on the lake, and no noise came from the cabins along the shore. As I pushed off, I was sitting at the stern, looking toward the bank. There was the cedar stump I'd wanted to tear down when we'd first come to the lake. Thankfully, Carol dissuaded me.

The stump, blackened by fire, had probably been created near the end of the 19th century, when the cedars along the shore had been harvested and taken to the mill in Shingleton. There's no telling how old it was, but, given the fact that it was fairly large and that cedars grow very slowly, it probably began its life as a seedling sometime in the middle of the 18th century, long before the wave of loggers swept across the Upper Peninsula.

I paddled slowly toward the south end of the lake, often pausing to let the canoe drift, listening to the morning sounds: the slight breeze in the trees, the distant caw of a crow, the occasional hum of a car's tires from the highway a mile away. Arriving at the sandy beach not far from Joe Lakosky's home, I turned the canoe around and faced up the lake.

If I angled a certain way, I couldn't see any of the docks along the eastern shore, only the trees to the west. This is what Crooked Lake must have looked like in the 1840s when William Burt and his party began their enormous task of surveying the Upper Peninsula. They were probably the first white people to see what they named Crooked Lake.

I wondered what Burt's thoughts were when he saw this little lake, one of over half a dozen in the immediate vicinity. I'm sure he wasn't thinking about vacation homes. He and his men had slogged through the trackless forest, skirting swamps, clambering over enormous deadfalls, battling mosquitoes and black flies, ending rainy days trying to start camp fires and dry soggy clothes. They probably just marked out the area, noting the bays and peninsulas and sketching in the swampy areas before moving on.

Burt, who'd invented an early version of the typewriter, had also invented a solar compass, which became an essential surveying tool in the Upper Peninsula, where there were so many iron ore deposits. But on cloudy, rainy days, or when the sun was behind hills, this wonderful instrument wouldn't have been much help.

After he and his men had finished the job here, they headed north and later west. In September 1844, he found enormous quantities of iron near what is now Ishpeming, and his reports led to the great mining boom that made the UP one of the country's leading producers of iron ore.

From the south end of the lake, I paddled north and west to the point directly across from our cabin. Along with my fellow summer residents, I'd often wondered why nobody lived there and occasionally fantasized a post-lottery-win fortune that would allow me to build a mansion, with a lot of little cabins for my family and friends.

It turns out somebody had lived there—four thousand years ago. Our friend Deb told us that archaeological digs have unearthed artifacts from the early woodland period: pottery shards, fire-cracked rock, chips and flakes from stone tool making. She, herself, found what she thinks was a stone scraper.

Why had they come to this little lake—for fishing or hunting or was the blueberry harvest good on the point? Did they come here throughout the year or was this a summer place just as it is for me and my neighbors? And what did they do about the mosquitoes during rainy summers? If they came to the bank to look over the water at the rising sun, they'd have seen it come up where my cabin now stands.

I turned the canoe in the direction of where I imaged they'd gazed and headed for home. After nearly four decades, I consider myself a Crooked Lake old timer. But that morning, I realized that many more had come here before. I wish I knew more about Burt's visit and the early woodland people's stays.

Our wonderful little lake has a long, long history.

A Solstice Celebration

Whenever I'm at the lake in June, I always say I'm going to get up early to watch the sun rise on the longest day of the year. But, it would be too rainy, or too windy, or too foggy to take the canoe out on the lake. Once, the weather was supposed to be fine, but I forgot to set the alarm. Another time, I'd celebrated solstice eve so well and late that I didn't hear it buzzing.

This year, I made it!

In the gray of predawn, I slipped the canoe into the water, paddled a couple of dozen strokes and then let the boat glide. Behind me on the shore, a robin chirped and a squirrel scolded. In the trees to the north crows quarreled, and, far to the south, the raucous cries of sand hill cranes carried on the breeze. To the west, the solstice full moon (there won't be another until close to my 150th birthday) dropped slowly toward the dark tree line. I paddled along the pathway of its broken reflection, gliding every two or three strokes to listen to the chorus of frog croaks and squeaks ahead.

A couple of hundred feet from the western shore I stopped paddling and drifted, watching the moon set and looking over my shoulder for signs of the rising sun. After a few minutes, the tops of the trees became bathed in a pale gold and soon the canoe was as well.

I turned and began to paddle home as quietly as I could. Our side of the lake was still in deep shadow, but not so deep that I couldn't see that I had an early morning companion. A solitary loon swam a hundred feet away from me, occasionally glancing over to make sure I wasn't getting too close. Just before I reached the dock, he disappeared under water, no doubt seeking breakfast. I tied up the canoe, went up to the cabin, poured a cup of coffee, and began to cook my breakfast.

Then I turned on the iPad and saw pictures friends had taken of last night's solstice sunset. Because of its being Leap Year, the longest day was yesterday, June 20th. I had missed it again! Even so, it was a great experience. Sharing it with the loon made it even better.

The Big Swim

At 11:57 this morning, I arrived at the corner of Elm and Superior in downtown Munising, 22.7 miles from my cabin. It took me 37 days to get here. That's because I swam all the way.

In case you think I'm losing it, let me explain. A few years ago, one of my friends, an inveterate walker, told me that, during his daily strolls, he'd walked the equivalent of the nearly two thousand miles from his residence in Edmonton, Alberta, to his boyhood home in San Diego, California. "I'd started to get bored with my walks, so, to make things more interesting, I kept track of my mileage each day and marked it on an Automobile Club map I had of the western states and Canadian provinces. It took me a year and a half to get to San Diego." Unless the temperature was well below zero or the pavement icy, he walked every day except Sunday.

"Why don't I do that from the cabin to Munising?" I thought. "Except by swimming, not walking." I'd been swimming "laps" along the lakeshore for several summers, but it often got pretty boring. Having a goal might give me some incentive to get in the water every day. I staked out 50 yards along the shore, from where the reeds grew to where the large trunk of a birch had fallen into the shallows. Eighteen round trips was a mile and, if I swam five times a week and did a little extra each day during the final week, I'd make Munising in about four weeks.

At first, things went swimmingly. At the end of the third day, I'd "swum" the three miles down the dirt road to the highway and had started north toward Shingleton, ten miles distant. But then things started to go downhill, you might say. For two days, the wind blew from the north, so I went like a torpedo heading one way, but it was all uphill the other way, and I made less than half my daily quota. In the middle of the second week, a severe storm was forecast around noon. I hit the water early to get my laps finished before its arrival. But, the storm was early too. As I swam by the dock, I saw two of my neighbors yelling and pointing up the lake. Dangerous dark clouds were rushing toward me and there was lightning in them. I sprinted to shore and raced to the cabin, took a long shower and found I'd forgotten how many laps I'd swum.

Then there was the day we all went on an excursion to Marquette— by car. I thought we'd be back by mid-afternoon and that I'd be able to get my laps in before dinner. But I hadn't factored in three hours shopping at WalMart. We got home too late to swim, and the next day I was too exhausted to even think of going near the water. By the end of the second week, I'd fallen four miles behind schedule.

The third week went well, until Friday. It was a sunny, calm early afternoon when I headed down to the lake. I waved at the neighbors on their dock and struck out for the reeds. As I stood up by the reeds to turn around, they called me. It seemed they had enjoyed a late brunch, were in the process of finishing a large pitcher of mimosas and needed my help. Being a good neighbor, I happily obliged, swum over to their dock, and forty-five minutes later walked home. I didn't add the half-lap to my total.

There followed several days of severe northerlies and a few when I suffered attacks of lethargy. I was well past my four week schedule and eight miles from Munising. And so, on the last week of the season, I turned up the pressure, averaging over a mile-and-a-half daily, refusing to let north winds, lethargy or mimosas prevent me from arriving, puffing and wheezing, in town.

I arrived just before the sun was over the yardarm.

What to do now? It was too late in the summer to consider swimming back home. So I waved to my neighbors who were back on their dock, waded ashore, stumbled to the cabin and, after I'd showed and dressed, took a bottle of bubbly and pitcher of orange juice out of the fridge, gathered four plastic champagne glasses, and headed to my dock. I called them over and we celebrated my successful arrival at the corner of Elm and Superior in Munising.

Aqua-Dogs

It is really fun sharing our place with the dogs. In the over years we've been coming to Crooked Lake, we've brought many of them with us. They've liked dashing into the woods when we walked the back road, they've staked out a claim on the old couch on the screened porch, and they've never wandered off when the dinner hour approached.

But, because we spend so much time down at the lake, that has been their favorite place. When we first arrive, they all rush straight to the shore, lunge in and walk around lapping water furiously. Then they get out, bounce over to us, shake furiously, and roll in the sand.

They have all been water dogs, but each in his or her own way.

Kate, the golden, loved the canoe. When she saw me coming down the path with the paddle, she'd trot out onto the dock and stand next to where the canoe was tied, waiting for permission to jump in. She'd sit regally in the front, occasionally looking back at me, her lowly minion, taking her on her excursion. When we returned to the dock, she'd await the command to disembark, jump out, leap into the water, jump out, shake all over the nearest humans and roll in the sand.

Petunia (Tuna for short) had never seen water before she came to the lake. She walked out to the end of the dock and, thinking the water was solid, stepped onto it. When she surfaced, she looked very surprised. She stayed close to the shore after that, walking through the shallows looking for frogs, but never finding any. Of course, each time she came ashore she'd do the shake and roll.

Zoe got very nervous the first time she saw me wade into the lake. With every step, more and more of me kept disappearing. She whimpered, walked back and forth, and tentatively touched the water. When I came back to her, she was overjoyed. She soon got over her fear of the water and became the most dangerous of aqua-dogs: a rescuer dog. She'd swim out and paw at me until I had to come ashore and take her up to the cabin so that I could finish my swim.

When we went to pick up Hankie from the breeder, we mentioned the lake and she said, "He's a labradoodle; he'll love the lake." He did: he'd shove his head underwater and blow bubbles and then transform himself into a water gazelle, leaping over the waves created by passing boats. Unfortunately, he also liked the swampy area at the end of the lake and, if he wasn't on the leash, would disappear into the muck, reappearing like one of those seagulls after an oil spill. Thank goodness he didn't shake and roll until we got him back to our beach and sluiced him off.

Lito, the littlest dog, a 12-pound rescue pup, spent most of his time on the dock hiding under the deck chairs, especially when the shadow of a soaring bald eagle crossed over him. But when he got thirsty, he used go over to the stairs leading into the water, put his front paws on the top step and start lapping. That nearly did him in. One day, as his long, pink tongue dipped into the water, a bass surged from beneath the dock and lunged at what, to it, must have been a very big worm. The fish was unsuccessful; but Lito never drank from the lake again.

And then there was Essa. He was a rescue dog we named after a rambunctious hockey player and he lived a life of reckless abandon. For some reason, he never took to the water. But he had a thing for beach towels and bathing suits and would go down the path along the shore and come back with something he'd purloined from a neighbor's low-hanging clothes line. One day, it was the bottom half of a girl's bikini. He dropped it in front of me as if it were a wonderful gift. I put him into the house and walked along the shore surveying each clothes line looking for a bikini top that matched. When I found one, I tiptoed up to the line, clipped the bottom on it and beat a hasty retreat. I don't think anyone saw me.

Sometimes the shaking and rolling of our aqua-dogs gets annoying. But watching them frolic and cavort in the water is another of the many joys of lakeside living.

Diving Lessons

Late this morning, while the loons were in the middle of lake, showing their bewildered chicks how to dive, there was another lesson going on along the shore. A mother was teaching her four-year-old the basics of swimming. Lakes everywhere have for decades become classrooms where birds and children have learned the importance of surviving in the water. In the middle of the last century, my father wrote a column describing a similar scene:

Well out in Cigarmakers Bay, a mother and father loon—the genuine water birds—are teaching their youngster to dive. It's quite a performance. The three birds paddle close together. The low gutturals of duck talk drift across the water. Then the parent birds make their demonstration dives. That, too, is quite a performance. They drop their heads and shrug their shoulders, like a kid pulling off a jersey, and down they go.

The young loon appears to watch the technique carefully. For a moment, he's left alone on the surface. Then he drops his head and shrugs up his shoulders to submerge. Seconds later the two parent birds come to the surface yards away to the southeast. They look around

Fig. 7-2: Sand Hill Crane

and go into more duck-talk. Just when they seem to be getting worried over junior, the young loon surfaces. Only he's yards away to the northeast. He bobs up and starts talking, probably saying, "By golly, I've made it," and he's so pleased to come up that he doesn't seem embarrassed at all over the direction he's taken.

The old birds swim over to him, maybe telling him where he went wrong and how he should learn to know where he's going underwater. The small loon, who looks a mite slap-happy, makes with the "sure, sure" routine and they do it all over again. Ma and Pa lift up, surge over and go down. Junior does likewise. Ma and Pa come up some distance away in the direction in which they're heading. Junior comes up miles off again. But what would you expect from a young loon?

Closer to shore, two humans are teaching their youngster to dive off a springboard. They cluck at him and explain the takeoff, the air balance and the entry. One of them goes up on the plank and gives a demonstration. It isn't a very good demonstration. The guy's getting old and rusty. But it should teach the youngster the rudiments. Pa comes up making duck sounds of encouragement and instruction. Junior wavers on the end of the board and takes off. He does about everything wrong and the procedure is repeated.

There's a considerable difference between the human and the bird. The young loon will learn how to dive and dive well. If he doesn't, he'll be mighty hungry. The boy on the springboard won't go hungry whether or not he masters his take-off, flight and entry. And the bird parents are good teachers, though looney.

Victoria Daily Times, July 24, 1951

The North Wind Doth Blow

It's frequently quite breezy down at the water. And that's a good thing because it keeps the Yooper Air Force (mosquitoes in the morning and horse flies in the afternoon) grounded. But, when the wind comes from the north, it keeps us all grounded. The water gets white-cap rough; the temperature drops by several degrees. When the wind gets too strong, we leave the deck for a spot that's shielded by the trees.

That happened today. This morning, as I was canoeing along the southern shore of the lake, half a mile from our dock, the wind direction changed. To make it back home, I had to turn the canoe around, kneel down and paddle stern-forward. It was vigorous exercise.

A couple of hours later, I decided to swim my laps along the shore. I moved through the water with speeds greater than I'd achieved in my (not very) prime years when I was headed south. But going north, it was another matter. If someone had been timing me with a stopwatch, they'd probably have had to rewind it at least once.

The wind was about the same strength in mid-afternoon when I came down to the dock and opened my book. The pages fluttered a little and I had to pull my hat down tight. I'd finished a chapter, put the book down, and was looking around when I saw a paddle boat approaching rapidly from the north. There were two young girls paddling happily and laughing. They whizzed past the end of the dock waving hello. I returned to my book and, a chapter or so later, I heard splashing noises from along the shore to the south. It was the girls, stepping gingerly through the reeds, pulling the paddle boat behind them. "We paddled as hard as we could, but the boat wouldn't go north," they explained as they huffed and puffed toward their own dock. "We've never been out in a paddle boat before."

As the afternoon progressed, the wind strengthened. I retreated to the sheltered spot, but couldn't escape the increasingly chilly air blowing through the trees. I closed my book and headed to the cabin. A molded plastic chair tumbled across the clearing. Inside, I looked out as the waves grew in size. There were no boats on the lake. I thought about the girls and was glad that they were probably safely inside their cabin.

I remembered another incident involving the north wind and in-experienced boaters. The water craft on our little lake are pretty tame. There are kayaks and canoes, fishing punts and pontoon boats. Occasionally there's a boat with a powerful enough motor to tow youngsters shrieking happily as they cling to an oversized inner tube. And, very occasionally, there's a jet ski, going back and forth, back and forth like wolves pacing in zoos.

One day, a jet ski and pilot we'd never seen before spent much of the morning roaring back and forth, deviating occasionally to charge at the loon family, forcing them to dive. When he came out in the after-noon, the north wind had sprung up and he took great joy in steering in circles and wrestling his craft in the chop created when his wake met the rising waves. He let out yelps like a rodeo contestant clinging to the back of a bucking bronco. Tiring of this game and the loons having retired for the day, he raced to the southern end of the lake and into what we call the lagoon. It's covered with lily pads and flowers and is a favorite sunning spot for frogs. Beneath the lily pads, thick stems extend down to the murky bottom. It's fun to canoe or kayak there, but you've got to watch out for those stems.

"Oh, oh," Clare said, as the jet ski zoomed into the lagoon and out of our sight. Suddenly its roar stopped. There were a few pathetic chug, chugs as jet ski and driver reappeared from the short channel leading from the lagoon. Then two sputters followed by silence.

A few minutes later, he approached our dock, pushing his craft through the reeds against the waves. He wasn't smiling. As he passed us sitting on the dock watching his slow progress, he muttered an imprecation, and then angrily declared: "That place is dangerous. They should put a warning sign up there. It's going to cost me hundreds of dollars to get this fixed." Then he continued on his way, huffing and puffing against the wind.

We didn't see or hear him or his machine again. The lake returned to its normal quiet. The loons returned to their regular tour of the lake.

It's an ill north wind that blows no good.

A Beauteous Evening and a Wondrous Event

Last evening was, to quote the poet Wordsworth, "a beauteous evening, calm and free." The north wind had dropped to a gentle breeze. The sun broke through the clouds, glinting off the ripples and painting the birches a pale gold. The pontoon boats had all been berthed for the night, and the only sounds were a gentle rustling of the aspen leaves and the lap of water against the dock steps.

Then I heard and beheld a truly wondrous event.

Through the trees along the bank came the sound of a kayak paddle pushing the water and, accompanying it, a soft voice and a slightly burbled reply. Then, in an open space between the trees, a kayak appeared, moving slowly. In it, Danny held the paddle and in front of him sat his two-year-old daughter, wearing an oversized pink hat that clashed with her bright orange life jacket. She seemed to be regally enjoying her first kayak ride. She was Cleopatra floating majestically down the Nile, her father the boatman supplying the power.

On the dock next to mine stood two great-grandmothers, a grandmother, a mother, an aunt, and a girl cousin waving and smiling as they observed an important ritual of the lake: a tiny child making her first kayak voyage.

I remembered when Danny, then a little boy, had gone with his grandfather in the old rowboat, learning to use the oars as they headed to their favorite fishing spot. And I remembered when, at another lake long ago and far away, I was first allowed to take the little kayak my father had built beyond the shallows of the swimming beach and, years later, when my children first learned about boats from their grandfather.

It's a ritual that has taken place hundreds of times on countless lakes. But every time it occurs, there's a special quality about it, for the little person learning the joy of boats and water and for the older spectators, as they stand smiling and perhaps misty-eyed, feeling joy in the old ritual and remembering other times they'd been witness to it.

Signs of Change

On the return part of my morning walk to the bridge, I made notes in a little writing pad about the signs at the end of each of the nineteen driveways. Now in the late afternoon, I sat on the dock and looked over the notes, thinking about the people who'd been our Crooked Lake neighbors since we moved in on July 25, 1985.

Nine of the signs, including ours, bore the same names they had during our first summer at the lake. However, two of these names belonged to the current owners who, as children several decades ago, had been eager young participants in their parents' cabin construction. In one case, the cabin now belonged to a grandson.

Every year, grandchildren, and even the occasional great-grandchild of the "pioneers" return to what are now their ancestral "summer" homes to participate in the unchanging activities of summer: trying to catch fish with bent pins attached to string and baited with struggling worms; picking blueberries and eating most of them before their attention spans diminish; sitting around evening campfires, dodging the shifting smoke, burning marshmallows, and shivering as they listen to scary stories.

Several cabins had "left the family" as younger generations declined the chance to carry on traditions of old people who were too weary to maintain them or who had passed on. I remember Dorothy telling me, the spring after her husband had died, "Joe told me that the saddest thing was that he would never see Crooked Lake again." Some cabins had changed hands three times, a couple four.

Of the owners who were there when we'd first arrived, only John of Lot 9 still owns his place. The sign was still there, but there had been a drastic and very sad change. Two years ago, he experienced a reality that we had all imagined and feared: when he arrived one early May day, the cabin wasn't there. A large dump of heavy, wet spring snow had caused its collapse. The debris had been hauled away, and now all that was left was concrete pad and a shed with some summer chairs in it. If the family decides to rebuild, it will be the first new cabin at Crooked Lake since the 1950s.

In addition to the family names, some of the signs had names for the home. Lot 8, a large log cabin was called "Backacher Lodge." The name evoked the great physical labor when the parents and children used spring and fall weekends, along with summer vacations, to build from the ground up. "Twin Birch" celebrated the trees beside the drive and the two families that owned Lot 7. "Hodge Podge Lodge" reflected the happy chaos that presided over Lot 17, where every summer the owners, their children and grandchildren, their own mothers, and assorted cousins and their kids, set up tents, staked out space on the screen porch, and one time rented a trailer that slept six.

"Point Four" referred to the number of original owners at Lot 11. Originally, their names had been below the cabin name. When they decided to sell, they carefully interviewed the prospective owner to see if he were the right kind of person to take over the place. He was. The title remained, but the names were changed to those of young grandchildren who would soon be enjoying the sandy beach and shallow water. The family on Lot 13, grandchildren of original settlers whose ancestors had come from Sweden to work in the Upper Peninsula mines, has given their place the name "Tystnaden," meaning "quiet" or "peaceful."

For some time, we've been thinking that we need a new sign. After three-and-a-half decades, the five letters of our name have faded and the post is beginning to list. "It's time for a change," Clare said. "And let's have a name for our place on the new sign." We chose the Anishinaabe word "wanakiwin," meaning "peace."

After we'd decided, I paid a visit to our next door neighbor to find out where he'd had his sign made, a sign that prominently featured the name he'd chosen for the place: "Unplugged." He was a computer expert and had bought the cabin, he told us, to get away from it all. "Just a minute," he said. "I'll get the address and phone number for you." He went to a desk at the corner of the room and turned on his laptop.

Baseball at the Lake

A few summers ago, I sat on the dock listening to one of the best games I've heard in over six decades of listening to baseball. It wasn't on WNUB Newberry, the Upper Peninsula's "Voice of the Tigers," and it wasn't from the Escanaba station, which featured the voice of Bob Uecker, broadcaster for the Milwaukee Brewers. The sounds of the game were coming through the trees from the lot next door.

As near as I could tell, it was the championship game of the East Crooked Lake Fourth-of-July Tournament. It was also, I gathered, the only game of the tournament. Scheduled for two in the afternoon, it had been moved to the early evening because of heavy thunderstorms and the tiredness of four players who had driven four hundred miles from Crystal Lake, Illinois, to participate.

The contest was played on a field located between Cabin 17 and the shore that was smaller than a suburban backyard. Eleven players participated, five aside and one substitute. They ranged in age from seven to the late seventies.

There were two almost teenagers (one a soccer player, the other an aspiring fashion artist); two university students (one of whom, when he was a small boy, aspired to be a St. Louis Cardinals superstar; the other a ringer recruited from Indiana University); two husbands (one a high school football coach, the other a recently retired third baseman from a Chicago area over-40 league); two teachers (one of whom had been a champion middle-distance runner, the other a seasoned veteran of many East Crooked Lake tournaments); and two grandparents (both a little slower than they used to be at getting to first on a bunt, but both still real gamers). The seven-year-old was designated as the substitute for either team.

Listening to the sounds drifting through the trees, it was difficult to know who was winning, even who was at bat. There were lots of fans—a couple of curious neighbors and countless mosquitoes and black flies. And there was, if I interpreted the sounds I heard, a game delay. Not more rain, but a dog who wandered onto the field. His name was Tonka and, unlike the miniature construction toys, he wasn't tiny. In fact, he looked more like Harold Huge, the cartoon dog. When he sat down between the (non-existent) mound and the (pie) plate, there was no pitching around him.

Many interesting sounds came through the trees. Every member of each team was, it seemed, player, coach, and umpire, especially the recently retired over-40-league third baseman. "Come on Grandma, get him home," he exhorted. "That ball was into the trees—it was foul," he announced. "Don't swing at those sissy-assed pitches—make him throw to you."

At one point, after I'd heard the crack of the ball hitting the bat, I heard the ringer from Indiana run down the dock and jump into the water. "It was foul!" he exclaimed. "I thought I could get it before it hit the ground—I mean water. Boy, it's nice and cool here. Time out."

I don't know who won. In fact, I think the game sort of petered out when the aroma of grilling hamburgers began to drift across the playing field. But it was, and still is, the best game I ever listened to.

"I hope they play next year," I thought to myself. "If they do, I'll certainly tune in."

Excitement

"What do you do for excitement around here?" a long-ago visitor asked. He wasn't impressed with the fact that (at that time) there was no internet or that we couldn't get more than a single TV station without one of those enormous satellite dishes.

"Oh, we check every couple of days to see if the blueberries are getting riper, and each Friday we watch the sunset to see how many trees the sun has moved north or south since last Friday. Every ten years, after we've repainted the cabin, we sit in our chairs, drink Pabst Blue Ribbon, and watch the paint dry."

He didn't stay around for long.

He should have been here an hour after sunrise this morning. We had some real excitement. I heard what I thought was a rather loud motorboat coming down the lake, when, to my surprise, a small float plane, flying a couple of dozen feet above the water, passed in front of our lot. In all my years here, I'd never seen anything like it.

I put on my robe and ran toward the lake. I heard the plane banking; it turned around and flew back up the lake, this time not far above the tree line. "I wonder if it's in trouble," I thought. "If it goes down in the water, will I have to paddle the canoe to the plane and pull the pilot out of the cockpit? If it crashes into the trees, will I have to ride my bike down the path and pull people out of the burning wreckage?" I could see myself on this evening's national news. (We have a satellite dish now.)

No crash; no splash. So I fastened my robe tightly, walked back to the cabin and reheated my coffee in the microwave. The plane must have landed (watered?), for I heard it travelling slowly back down the lake. It turned around in front of our dock, the pilot ignoring my friendly wave, and putt-putted out of sight. It reappeared, this time airborne, barely cleared the tree line at the south end of the lake and disappeared. When I asked around later, no one had any information to offer.

This afternoon, I resumed my routine quest for excitement and checked to see how the blueberries were coming along; swam my laps along the shoreline, keeping a wary eye out for planes; and chopped some kindling. No watching paint dry, because we don't do the cabin again until next year.

Tonight, because it's Friday, I'll be at lakeside checking out which tree the sun sets behind. Then I'll go straight to bed. Too much excitement for one day.

8   September Songs

After they had become empty nesters, my parents used to spend their lake vacations in September, a time, my father told me that, had a "sweet-melancholy beauty that could break your heart." Both as a boy on Canada's West Coast and, until the last few years when I became a retired teacher, the sadness brought on by the fading of summer began a few days before Labor Day. Now, I frequently spend much of September at the lake. The sweet-melancholy still arrives, although more gradually. It is offset, however, by the enjoyment of new experiences of late summer and early autumn.

The Season's Flies

Each year I save the *Mining Journal* calendar that I've used to note the high and low temperatures and the general weather for each day and, when I was younger and much more energetic, the number of "laps" I'd swum along the lakeshore. It's fun to pull out a calendar from a decade or so ago and see what the summer was like.

We really don't need the calendar to tell us the progress of the seasons. All we have to do is note what kinds of flies are making our lives miserable.

In the warmer days of late May and early June, it's the black flies, small but bloodthirsty little devils who get under your skin (metaphorically) by getting under your clothing. If you haven't cleaned up the matted carpet of last year's leaves before their season arrives, you'd better wear a thick, long-sleeved shirt, jeans that are tucked into heavy woolen socks, and a hat with a screen covering for your face. They'll rise up in swarms when you pull the leaves away from the house and, when you lift the leaves into a wheelbarrow, they'll dart for the exposed flesh between the cuffs of your sleeves and your gloves.

In the gloriously hot (but not too hot) days of summer, as you stretch out on the dock enjoying the feel of the sun on your well-lotioned back, warming up enough to enjoy the deliciously cool water when you go for a swim, you encounter the next plague: the horse flies. Trying to escape them, you plunge into the lake, swim as many strokes as you can underwater, and come up to discover one circling just above your head.

She (I'm told that the females are the biters) follows you back to the dock. Wet bodies are, it seems, like marinated beef, and she settles on your arm seeking a select chunk of prime meat. But, if you're vigilant, here's your chance for revenge. She generally takes three or four seconds to make the selection and seems to focus her attention completely on that task. You quickly slap her, pick up the body and toss it into the water, chuckling maliciously as a passing fish darts to the surface to enjoy a fresh snack.

There are a couple of mid-summer flies we like. In fact, they are flies-in-name-only. Often as we dry off sitting at the dock, a dragonfly will come by, settle on an arm and lick the salt that's dried on it. We mutter rude words at the horse flies, but we're very polite to the dragonflies. We would be even if we didn't like them. When we were kids, we were told that they sewed up the mouths of people who swore. Of course, we now recognize that as faux science employed by parents, but still, it's better to be safe than sorry.

The other flies-in-name-only that we like aren't often found this far north in Michigan. Only on a very warm night after a very hot day do the fire flies appear, and then not many of them. Their numbers have decreased not just here, but everywhere. The causes: light pollution, habitat loss, and pesticides. My favorite firefly memory is of the time my sister was visiting from the west coast of Canada, where there are no fireflies. I'd just fallen asleep when a frightened voice came from the other room. "There's somebody coming up the trail!" she said. She was looking out the window at a firefly whose blinking light seemed to be heading toward the house.

Last night, I encountered the final and most dreaded flies of the season. It was a calm, quiet late evening and I was standing on the dock watching the sunset. After it had sunk behind the trees, my neighbor, who was standing on her dock, called softly: "Look how far south the sun has moved. It seems like only yesterday that we were watching it set at the north end of the lake. Where has the time gone?"

Where? I thought to myself, realizing that not long from now, I'd be starting the melancholy rituals of closing up for the season.

"Time flies," I replied across the water.

Fading Summer

It was 42 degrees outside when I woke up this morning, the coldest it had been since late May. When I walked out to the woodshed just after dawn to gather kindling and starter pieces for a morning fire, it was still dark. Dawn was arriving nearly an hour-and-a-half later than it had at the solstice.

Shortly after the rising sun had touched the birches and aspens across the lake, revealing more branches burnished with gold and red than had been there a few days ago, the loons swam down the lake. All were the same size and all dove with equal precision and came up at approximately the same spot. The chick was ready to leave its first home and fly to warmer waters. He would not return to Crooked Lake next year. As an adult he would have to find his own territory and a mate with whom to raise his offspring.

Fig. 8-1: The ubiquitous Purple Aster: a harbinger of Fall

As the dogs and I walked the back road, they found every puddle that had been created by last night's rain, part of one of the first storms of early autumn. Along the side of the road, purple asters had replaced the yellow daisies of summer. At the end of his driveway, a neighbor was clearing away a branch that had come down in the night. It had a few yellowed leaves on it.

Later that morning, as I walked down to the lake, a squirrel raced across the path, a pine cone in its mouth. There were no mosquitoes or flies to attack me. Out on the lake, an unfamiliar flock of bufflehead ducks paddled lazily, taking a brief rest on their journey from further north. I walked back to the house, noticing that the hummingbird who had fiercely defended the feeder was sharing it with others. I'd filled it only a couple of days ago and already it was half empty.

In the afternoon, I cycled along the back path, thinking I might find a blueberry bush with some fruit still on it. Instead I found the season's first blackberries. Swarms of little birds that had been gathering in recent days rose into the air as I pedaled past.

Later in the afternoon, it was warm and there was no wind. I decided to swim a few laps along the shore. But the water temperature had dropped considerably overnight. I called it quits after a couple of turns. The thermometer hanging in the water registered 64 degrees. Dressed, I returned to the dock to enjoy what was called a summer ale and remembered that, a couple of days earlier, the guy stocking the shelves at the grocery store told me that Oktoberfest would be available next week.

The sports segment on this evening's news was all about the Green Bay Packers' first game of the National Football Season. There was hardly a mention of baseball. Shortly after I'd finished a late dinner, the sun began to set. It had moved so far south that its rays shone horizontally onto the birches around the cabin, turning them almost a liquid gold.

After the sun disappeared, it quickly grew cold. I retreated indoors, built a small fire, and, as I watched the flames dancing, began to review the events of the day. As I did, three snippets of poetry floated into my mind. The first were the opening lines from a poem by Rachael Field: "Something told the wild geese/ It was time to fly./ Summer sun was on their wings,/ Winter in their cry." The signs of departure were all around the lake.

Then I remembered having heard the sound of an oven bird, also known as a teacher bird, this afternoon, and thought of the closing line of Robert Frost's sonnet about that late summer bird: "What to make of a diminished thing." I found an answer when I remembered these famous lines from Andrew Marvell's poem, "To His Coy Mistress." "Though we cannot make our sun / Stand still, yet we will make him run."

The speaker of Marvell's poem wasn't talking about the fading of summer; but the words could apply. Each evening the sun would be setting farther south on the tree line across the lake. But before I, like the wild geese, decided it was time to go, there were so many wonderful things to enjoy: a trip to Peninsula Point to see the monarch butterflies gathering for their long journey to Mexico; another to Kingston Plains, where the acres of large stumps bore silent testimony to the logging era of the late 19th century; morning canoe trips along the lake, smelling the wood smoke from someone's cabin and noticing the daily change of colors; evenings on the dock, sipping an Oktoberfest and listening to the quiet; and drifting to sleep lulled by the gentle night noises outside the window.

Labor Day 1951

On Labor Day weekend, no matter how sunny the days or warm the water, my cousins, my sisters and I would moon about, disconsolately realizing that "this time" in three ... two ... one days, we'd be in school. On Sunday, our cousin Michael and his family would leave the lake in the early morning for their home on the mainland. The next morning, Wendy and Brian, who lived in Victoria, would also depart. Sheri, Gael, and I would be left, grudgingly helping with camp cleanup and close-up, occasionally swimming, but taking little joy in it. Here's how my father described the mood in the column published the day after Labor Day:

Our voices sounded a little too loud as we took the boat out of the water yesterday. We were telling each other we needn't pull it up tonight. We'd be using it again, going out to summer camp to fish this month and the next.

There'd be lots more weekends at the lake before we closed up for the winter. The sleeping bags would be snug enough when the weather turned cold, and there was plenty of wood cut for the fire. We knew all that. There wasn't much reason to keep repeating it. But we did. We were trying to talk ourselves around the sadness that comes at the end of summer. In its way it was good, brave talk, only it didn't carry conviction. Nobody was fooled.

Even young Peter, who came in August to the camp next door, shared the feeling. He had arrived with a yell for a greeting and he'd been quiet only when he slept. He'd been alternately a Indian, a plainsman, and, occasionally, the most talkative fisherman on the Island during August. Yesterday, though, there didn't seem to be any fight in him. And since his cowboy outfit was packed, he couldn't be expected to let go with a "yippee." It was a changed boy who came over to bid us farewell, an unusually quiet youngster who shook hands with an unaccustomed formality. There wasn't any swagger to his shoulders as he turned away and plodded toward the small car, all packed and ready for the highway that would take it to the Nanaimo ferry. We'd kidded the boy on his exuberance during the summer. There was something too sensitive to stand a kidding as he left.

You could sense the same reaction in the rest of the small fry. There were protests from them as the springboard came down and was packed away under the shack for the season. It was the same board they'd refused to dive from during the summer, the same one they'd hoped would break when you asked them to try a jack-knife. Still, when it left its stand and was pushed between the floor joists, they objected.

Small girls looked on in resentment as the tent, sun-dried and weathered, came down to be stowed away. This they had taken to be their own. Under it they had raised their playtime families. On its ropes they had hung endless lines of doll's washing. By its walls, they had cooked innumerable meals, carefully mixed of sand and mud and garnished with pebbles in their toy dishes. They stood a little indignant, a little challenging, tenants evicted from a home they'd made.

Up at the shack, the melancholy job of cleaning up for the season went on. A summer's collection of trifles was gathered together from the windowsills and the boxes on the floor. The smooth white stone that came from the bottom of the lake and which a very somber young man had explained was a pearl of great value was tossed again into the water. The big matchbox full of dried rushes, cut to cigarette length, went into the stove, glowing as the "smokes" had never glowed between the lips of young sophisticates. The shotgun made from a broomstick and a narrow wedge of shiplap was tossed aside, and with it assorted feathers that had been an Indian's head-dress.

You felt a little mean, carrying on the clean-up, and you knew how the youngsters were feeling when you pulled up the boat in the evening. You heard the crickets chirping in the stillness and then you wandered out to the car, quiet, like young Peter as he headed for the Nanaimo ferry.

Victoria Daily Times, September 4, 1951

No Labor Day Blues

The weather is gloomy at Crooked Lake today, the Saturday of Labor Day weekend. The water is steel gray; there is no sunlight to highlight the waves stirred up by a west wind. Thunderstorms and rain are forecast for later this afternoon, But it's not gloomy to me. I'm not going back to school on Tuesday, either as a teacher or a pupil. For the first time since I started summering in the UP over four decades ago, I'll be spending all of September here.

There will be very few other people around. But I certainly won't be bored... there's so much I'm looking forward to doing. There are some outside chores I've put off: touching up the paint where it's peeling around the windows, raking the leaves way back from the cabin, and cutting the lower branches off the hemlocks and pines (not just to make the place look neater but to reduce the fire hazard), cleaning windows that are in danger of becoming opaque.

I'm going to revisit the places we frequently take our visitors to: Fayette Historic Park (the site of a long-ago smelting operation); the boardwalk through the Sandy Point Marsh near Munising (where strollers can look closely at local plants); and downtown Marquette (where a person can gaze at historical buildings, purchase wonderful books at Snowbound, and enjoy fine local beer and food at the Vierling). I'm also planning to visit a place I've never gone to before and always said "next year:" Grand Island. Just off Munising Bay, it was settled long ago by the Anishinaabe people and later by traders. In the earlier 20th century, it was owned by one of the timber barons, who set it up as his private hunting reserve, complete with imported game and a log-sided lodge that still looks out over Lake Superior.

I'm going to enjoy the quiet and the solitude. But I'll also be entertaining. One night I'll invite one of my neighbors (he's my age and first spent summers at the lake when he was a young teenager) for our annual spaghetti dinner. We'll share news about our grown children and grandchildren and compare what it was like spending summers at a lake during the primitive 1950s. Then, a few days before I close up, I'll have a visit from a friend I haven't seen for over thirty years. We'd shared our love of children's literature and she joined me as part of the hockey broadcast team at Western Michigan University. We've had lots of life experiences since then and so we'll have lots to catch up on.

So, this Labor Day weekend, I'm not gloomy. There's so much to look forward to in the waning days of summer.

Peninsula Point: Butterfly Rendezvous

Just after lunch on Labor Day, I saw the season's first "snowbird." It wasn't a tundra swan resting on the lake during the long journey to its winter home. And it wasn't a car with Florida plates owned by two retired Yoopers driving to a place where they could play golf all year around.

It was a monarch butterfly.

As I walked down to the shore, he fluttered ahead of me and landed on a goldenrod. (I knew it was he by the two black spots on the back wings.) He rested a few minutes, taking nectar from the flowers before flying straight across the lake. I didn't know where he'd come from, but I had a pretty good idea where he was going. In a few days, he'd be joining other monarchs at Peninsula Point, which juts out into Lake Michigan east of Escanaba. After a journey of many weeks, he'd be arriving in the Sierra Madre Mountains of Mexico, his "snowbird" destination.

A couple of days later, I drove to Peninsula Point on my last day trip of the season. I caught frequent glimpses of Little Bay de Noc to my right before entering a cedar forest which, I'm told, is like the one at the butterflies' final destination. The road ended in a clearing surrounded on three sides by Lake Michigan, which sparkled in the morning sun. On the point stood the square tower of Peninsula Point Lighthouse, built in 1865, decommissioned in 1936, and now listed on the National Register of Historic Places.

A couple of dozen adults and children, along with a few leashed dogs, wandered in the field and along the shoreline. Many people were pointing cameras at the trees, bushes, and clumps of goldenrod. Several monarchs fluttered in the air above them. Others were gathering nectar from the flowers, fuel for their long journey ahead. A few were still

Fig. 8-2: The Magnificent Monarch Butterfly

clinging to the branches of the cedars, looking like tiger-striped autumn leaves.

Some of these magnificent winged creatures had summered nearby. More have come from other parts of the eastern and central UP. It's reported that many have blown in from the Canadian shores of Lake Superior.

"A few minutes ago," a lady with a camera with a very long lens aimed at a cedar branch remarked, "a dozen or so flew into the air and took off south." They were beginning a miraculous journey across the lake to Wisconsin and then cross-country to Mexico. Unlike their summer predecessors, whose life span does not usually exceed six weeks, these butterflies, the last-born of the season, will not die until they reach their winter destination and breed the first of several generations that will make their way north come spring.

The next morning, I spotted another monarch on a stock of goldenrod swaying beside the path to the lake. When it fluttered off into the distance, I was about to say, "See you next year!" as I do to the loons and the migrating ducks when I close up each summer. Instead, I called out, "See your great-great-great grandchildren next summer."

I sat on the dock, gazing out at the tree line over which the solitary monarch had flown, thought about "ever-returning spring," and felt a deep reverence for the wondrous regenerative powers of nature.

DIRECTIONS: Take highway US-2 three miles east from Rapid River, then turn south on country road 513 and proceed 17 miles to Peninsula Point.

September Showers, Autumn Winds

The English poet John Keats referred to autumn as the "season of mists and mellow fruitfulness." In September there are plenty of morning mists in the UP, but not much mellow fruitfulness unless you happen to have an apple tree in your backyard, which I don't. There can be wonderful warm, sunny days, when you can walk, canoe, or just sit without worrying about flies or mosquitoes.

Yesterday, started as one of those days. But by late morning, the clouds had moved in, and by mid-afternoon, it was raining heavily and steadily. The people still at the lake welcomed the change in the weather grudgingly. We loved what used to be called "Indian Summer" (which turns out to have been a prejudiced term), but the ground was becoming very dry.

Then, today, the first nor'wester of the season swept across the bay. The lake was a leaden gray except for the whitecaps frothed up by the wind. When the sun made a brief appearance from behind the clouds scudding across the sky, it had no warmth. Leaves, which little over a day earlier had been floating lazily down in the sunlight, now flew against the window, driven by the gusts. A plastic Adirondack chair tumbled across the grass in front of the cabin. The top half of a rotten birch thudded down across the trail.

It was clearly not the day for what I'd planned as the last canoe trip of the summer. Instead, when the wind dropped somewhat I walked along the lakeside trail in front of the cabins.

And I noticed what wasn't there.

The flags, which had stood sentinel during the summer, day and night and through all kinds of weather, had been taken from their dock-end posts, folded and put away to await the late May return of the cabin owners. Most of the docks, too, had disappeared, dragged in sections well above the high-water level.

Fig. 8-3: Final farewells

Children's colorful sand pails that had usually been scattered along the narrow beaches like large summer flowers had vanished; the blue, green, red, and yellow kayaks that had dotted the banks were now stored in sheds. Baskets of red, purple, and white petunias no longer hung from hooks outside now boarded-up screen porches.

Along with them had disappeared the slapping of screen doors, the shrieking of children dashing into chilly waters, the quiet evening conversations between fishermen as their boats putted softly past the cabins. Soon, the leaves of maples, birches and aspens will have fallen, leaving the branches of the trees across the lake bare. Crooked Lake would go into hibernation.

But the memories of a summer that has been fading since Labor Day will not wither and fall. They will remain evergreen, taken by cabin residents to their winter homes. And they will carry with them the promise of lakeside joys that will be reborn next year.

Closing Up

> "Close-up time marked the death of the season and we
> wondered if there'd be any seasons like it to follow."
> *Victoria Daily Times*, September 20, 1955

There are only a few yellow leaves on the trees across the lake; the loons departed several days ago; all but two of the other summer residents have departed; the days are half an hour shorter than the nights. The hunting season is moving into full swing.

Like the geese in Rachel Field's poem, "Something told the wild geese," I now know "it is time to go." And so I have begun the week-long ritual countdown of closing up the cabin. Although I'm doing in reverse many of the same actions I did when I opened up in late spring, actions I've done for many seasons, they lack the joy and excitement of the rituals of May. I find myself afflicted with a kind of melancholy lethargy.

My first act in preparation for departure may seem unusual. I check the home game schedule of the Green Bay Packers. If they are playing on either Sunday or Monday, I don't leave then. The traffic the day before and all the day of the game will be extremely heavy. And if I want a motel an hour or so past Lambeau Field, I might as well forget it.

I book my favorite motels, the ones with outside doors and places nearby to walk the dogs. I try to make sure my final overnight stop is somewhere only six or seven hours from Albuquerque. I don't want to be on the highway between Santa Fe and Albuquerque any time after mid-afternoon, when the 55-mile stretch turns into a straight version of the Indianapolis speedway.

Next I establish stop dates for the newspaper, mail, long distance service, and internet and make a call to Dave the plumber to come in next week to winterize the water system. I set aside the clothes I'll need on the trip and the ones that still have at least another winter of city life in them. The others I'll use this week and leave behind in their retirement home.

Then I carefully begin the most choreographed activity of closing up. I begin to "eat down" or, as a friend joked, to "eat myself out of house and home." Over the summer I'd established a cache of frozen leftovers ("tovers" the kids used to call them, wrinkling their noses as they did so). I've purchased just enough fresh stuff—meat, produce, milk, and eggs—to supplement the frozen surprises in the fridge. And I stocked up on just enough craft beer to have a couple left for my final evening on the dock. If I've planned carefully, there will be only a heel of bread, a swig of milk, and a bit of wilted salad to put in the last bag of trash I take to the dumpster.

On the day before departure, I bring in the heavy lawn and dock furniture, put up the support beams in the living room, and make my farewell tours, first in the canoe on Crooked Lake and then on the bike to Colwell Lake. I pack the car, chop enough kindling and starter wood for the first fires of next year, take a plunge in the chilly lake, and crunch on a couple of pieces of micro-waved pizza. I sit on a bench on the dock, enjoying the last craft beer of the season as the sun enters the final stage of its descent.

My final act before going to bed is to pack a special box, the metaphorical one in which I place the tapestry of memories, of canoe and bike rides, of visits with friends, of watching the loons, and of sitting quietly on the dock or in front of the fire. These will sustain me in my months in the city of the pavements gray, until, one day in late winter, I'll start dreaming of trails and counting sleeps.

Envoi

The electric and telephone cords have been disconnected and all the switches in the fuse box flipped to off. The windows have been tightly closed, latched and covered by curtains. The cabin doors are all locked. Everything that's going home is snugly packed in the car. The dogs, fearful of being left behind, bound into it excitedly.

I move slowly down the path to the dock. The smell of a distant morning fire drifts through the trees; a small brown bird flits from branch to branch; mist rises from the lake. The rays of the early morning sun illuminate the birches, popples, and maples on the far shore. Branches of scarlet or gold contrast with the deep greens of pine, hemlock and cedar. Two swans, overnight visitors on their way south, float majestically along the distant shore. On the bank by the dock, golden rod, yellow saw thistles, purple asters and white turtleheads, the flowers of autumn, sway in the gentle breeze that begins to ripple the water.

"Goodbye, lake," I call out, feeling a sadness welling up. I touch the gnarled trunk of the "Tom Thomson tree," Carol's favorite. Its branches are nearly bare of needles; it may not last many more seasons.

"I'll see you next year," I murmur softly.

"I hope."

I walk quickly to the car and begin the long drive to the city of the pavements gray.

Afterword

At the beginning of this century, I spent several weeks at the family cabin at Shawnigan Lake on the West Coast of Canada, the place where I had, half a century earlier, enjoyed the endless summers of childhood. I was there to unwind after a long and stressful winter and to begin collecting the columns my father had, over a 24-year period, written for the local newspaper. Twice a week, after enjoying my morning coffee while looking out the window at the lake, I'd make the 26-mile drive into Victoria, where I'd scan reels of newspaper files at the public library and make copies of those pieces I thought would be of interest to members of my family. In the late afternoon, I'd sit at the lakeshore enjoying the warmth of the sun, gazing again at the water and the hill rising on the other side of the lake, and thinking about the columns I'd copied.

Many of the columns were about Shawnigan Lake: the passage of the seasons from Easter, when we opened up, to Canadian Thanks-giving (October), when we closed; the activities of children, dogs, birds and squirrels; the joys of fishing; memories of earlier years at the lake. What I was experiencing at lakeside, I was also reading descriptions of in his writings.

A recently retired English professor, I found myself noticing not just what he was writing about, but how he was writing it: the events he chose, the details he selected, the words he used to capture the events and communicate them to others.

Again influenced by my career of teaching and writing about English literature, I realized that what he presented in his 600 to 800 word essays were almost what the English poet William Wordsworth in "The Prelude" referred to as "spots of time." These were moments that had what the poet called "a renovating virtue" which, when recalled, nourished and repaired our souls. Many of my father's lake pieces were created after spending weekends and summer or fall vacations away from the newsroom. Others were retrospective pieces, musings on memories. In them he chose words that would recreate for his readers these moments of watching and listening.

On a late May day a few years ago, I was reading a collection of my father's columns that I'd brought to the Little Cabin in the Big Woods when I looked out the window at the lake. A couple of loons were swimming by. As I watched, I thought it would be fun to write about them and began wondering how my father would have described them. That afternoon, I wrote a few hundred words about the birds in a spiral notebook. Over the next few weeks, I filled it with other short entries—some written immediately after I'd seen something at the lake that I'd found interesting; others, weeks or months later when the incidents had become memories. During the following summers, I filled more notebooks with moments, memories and musings.

The short pieces in these notebooks became the basis for many of the essays in *Summers at the Lake.* As I selected, combined, expanded, and revised these journal entries and created new essays, all about the length of my father's columns, I had two revelations. The first was that, nearly 30 years after he'd died (while doing chores around the old family cabin), he was mentoring me. I often found myself thinking, "How would he have said this?" and used the imagined answers to guide me. I also came to understand the old saying that, as they grow older, sons often become their fathers. If this were the case with me, I would be very happy, and I think my father would have been pleased.

Acknowledgements

This collection of essays would not have been possible without the welcome assistance of many people. Thank you to Victor Volkman of Living History Press, who encouraged me to undertake this project and guided me with patience and wisdom along the way. To editor Bob Rich goes my gratitude for his fine work. He not only spotted my many typos but offered valuable suggestions on how to clarify my writing. Deb Le Blanc, whose wonderful photographs grace *Summers at the Lake*, has for well over four decades, helped me and my family discover the many hidden wonders of the UP. The *Times-Colonist* of Victoria, Canada granted me permission to include several of my father's 1950s newspaper columns from the *Victoria Daily Times*. To my UP friends Sharon, Brenda, Norm and Kerry, thank you for your support and encouragement over the years. My Crooked Lake neighbors added greatly to my enjoyment of my extended Crooked Lake summers. And finally to Clare and Alberto and to Carol -- the Little Cabin in the Big Woods would not have been so wonderful a place without you.

About the Author

Jon C. Stott, Professor Emeritus of English at the University of Alberta, has spent most of his summers beside lakes – as a boy at Shawnigan Lake on Vancouver Island, Canada, and, since 1971 (when he was a professor at Western Michigan University), at lakes in Michigan's Upper Peninsula. Since his retirement, he has written non-academic books about minor league professional sports and the craft beer boom, along with retellings of traditional legends and folktales. The stories in *Paul Bunyan in Michigan: Yooper Logging, Lore & Legends* are set in the Upper Peninsula of Michigan. He is currently writing a celebration of and guide to the craft breweries and brewpubs of the Upper Peninsula.

Photo credit: Clare K. Stott

About the Photographer

Deb Le Blanc, a retired plant ecologist, worked forty years for the United States Forest Service on the Hiawatha National Forest. Since early childhood, she has spent every summer at the family cabin beside the Indian River in the central Upper Peninsula. During her childhood years, she gained a passion for the out-of-doors and photography. She has restored the family cabin into a year round home where she lives with her family of furry kids, who often join her exploring the vast beauty of the Upper Peninsula.  When kayaking, she can be seen with her beloved American Eskimo dog Kyna sitting on the bow of her kayak.

Index

CPSIA information can be obtained
at www.ICGtesting.com
Printed in the USA
BVHW022058280422
635575BV00001B/1

9 781615 996698